the MITSITAM CAFE *cookbook*

Recipes from the
SMITHSONIAN NATIONAL MUSEUM
of the
AMERICAN INDIAN

Richard Hetzler

Foreword by Kevin Gover

Introduction by Nicolasa I. Sandoval

Food photographs by Renée Comet

Smithsonian
National Museum of the American Indian

Washington, D.C., and New York,
in association with
Fulcrum Publishing
Golden, Colorado

The National Museum of the American Indian, Smithsonian Institution, is committed to advancing knowledge and understanding
of the Native cultures of the Western Hemisphere, past, present, and future, through partnership with Native people and others. The
museum works to support the continuance of culture, traditional values, and transitions in contemporary Native life. The museum's
publishing program seeks to augment awareness of Native American beliefs and lifeways and to educate the public about the history
and significance of Native cultures.
www.AmericanIndian.si.edu

Smithsonian
National Museum of the American Indian

Associate Director for Museum Programs: Tim Johnson (Mohawk) • Publications Manager: Tanya Thrasher (Cherokee)
Project Editor: Sally Barrows • Recipe Editor: Carolyn Miller • Food Styling: Lisa Cherkasky, Bruce Barnes

Library of Congress Cataloging-in-Publication Data
Hetzler, Richard.
 The Mitsitam Cafe cookbook : recipes from the Smithsonian National Museum of the American Indian / Richard Hetzler ;
foreword by Kevin Gover ; introduction by Nicolasa I. Sandoval ; food photographs by Renée Comet.
    p. cm.
 "National Museum of the American Indian, Smithsonian Institution, Washington, D.C."
 Includes bibliographical references and index.
 ISBN 978-1-55591-747-0 (hardcover)
1. Indian cookery. 2. Cookery, American. 3. Mitsitam Cafe. I. National Museum of the American Indian (U.S.) II. Title.
TX715.H5736 2010
641.59'2--dc22
                    2010014945

Printed in China
0 9 8 7 6 5 4 3 2

Design: Margaret McCullough, Corvus Design Studio, www.corvusdesignstudio.com
Cover photo: Fiddlehead Fern Salad, © Renée Comet, Restaurant Associates, and Smithsonian Institution
Back cover photos: Roasted Venison, Hibiscus Agua Fresca, Cranberry Crumble, Cedar-Planked Fire-Roasted Salmon,
© Renée Comet, Restaurant Associates, and Smithsonian Institution. Photo of Christopher Cote (Osage) with fry bread,
author photo, © Smithsonian Institution

Fulcrum Publishing
4690 Table Mountain Drive, Suite 100
Golden, Colorado 80403
800-992-2908 • 303-277-1623
www.fulcrumbooks.com

For my mother, Debra Hetzler,
who taught me what passion for cooking really is,
and for my children, Raven Hetzler and Tarah Hetzler,
whose smiles give me the drive to always do better and learn more.

Contents

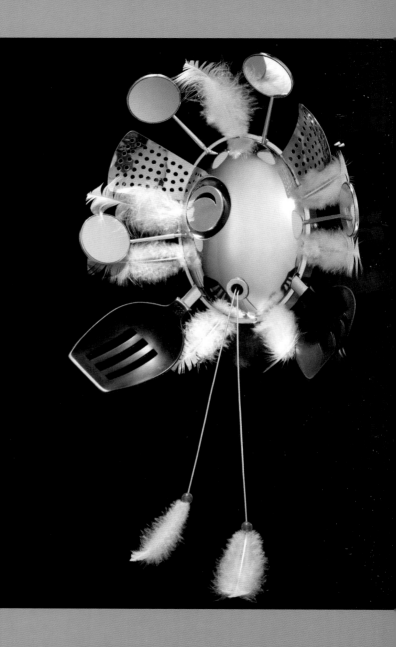

FOREWORD

In sharing our familiar foods, we share our cultures in a vital, daily way. Our food choices and ways of obtaining and preparing food powerfully influence our sense of community. Even for contemporary city and suburban dwellers, the family dinner table, the line at the grocery store, the fast-food lunch are all rituals that shape our daily lives and, by extension, our culture.

For Native peoples, the ceremonies surrounding hunting, gathering, growing, harvesting, and cooking food were for thousands of years necessarily part of a close, intricate relationship with the land. Foods and preparation techniques were adapted to the cycles of the weather and the contours of specific environments. Northern Plains hunters efficiently took bison by herding them off the edge of the region's rocky bluffs. Native farmers of the Eastern Woodlands region devised the system, beneficial to all three crops, of planting corn, beans, and squash together in mounds. And all Native cultures honored the land, water, and sky for their power and abundance.

Despite the centuries of upheaval that Europeans inflicted on Native peoples, this relationship with the land, and with specific foods, resonates deeply in Native communities today. Most of the meals that accompany ceremonies, dances, powwows, funerals, and festivals feature at least one traditional dish as part of a more contemporary menu. In southeast Alaska, street vendors sell smoked salmon at the Tlingit, Haida, and Tsimshian festival called Celebration. The Tohono O'odham of Arizona prepare chile stew,

tortillas, squash, and corn for Days of the Dead feasts in honor of departed family members. In my own Pawnee community, we make corn soup to accompany our meat, fry bread, and fruit at almost every tribal ceremony and event.

Before 1492, tomatoes, potatoes, wild rice, salmon, pumpkins, peanuts, bison, chocolate, vanilla, blueberries, and corn, among many other foods, were unknown in Europe, Africa, and Asia. Today, we think of tomatoes as an Italian staple, of potatoes as quintessentially Irish or northern European, and even of peanuts as native to Africa. But Native American farmers cultivated and developed these foods over hundreds of generations, long before Europeans exported them throughout the world.

During the past decade, "eating locally" has become a self-conscious act, an endeavor in and of itself. In farmers' market terms, eating locally most often means eating foods that have been grown or raised within a hundred miles of where we live. But

Larry Beck (Chnagmiut Yup'ik, 1938–1994). Tunghak Inua, 1982. Seattle, Washington. Mask made of a plastic slotted spoon, metal straining spoon, dental mirrors with Indian head on reverse, and feathers radiating from the back of a vehicle mirror, 32.8 x 23.5 x 7 cm. 25/5410

foods that are truly local are indigenous to specific regions and adapted (whether naturally or by a farmer's efforts) to a specific landscape. These are the foods that became as fundamental to indigenous cultures as song, dance, story, art, and ceremony.

Essential to survival, food is also an expression of our family, community, and cultural values. In every Native community, there are recipes so familiar they have never been written down and simple dishes that appear on the table at every gathering. In sharing these dishes with each other and our guests, we share our stories in the most ordinary yet significant way. It was therefore natural that in planning the National Museum of the American Indian, we gave a good deal of thought to the food we would provide our visitors. Divided into serving stations representing five general cultural landscapes in North and South America, the Mitsitam Native Foods Cafe (*mitsitam* means "let's eat" in the local Piscataway and Delaware languages) allows our visitors to experience Native cultures and indigenous foods in ways that appeal to all the senses, transcending the limits of a museum exhibition.

With all of the cafe's dishes based on indigenous American ingredients or cooking techniques, the restaurant—and chef Richard Hetzler in particular—has adapted traditional foods to the requirements of a modern cafeteria. Visitors can see their tamales being made by hand and their salmon roasting on an open fire pit—both ancient techniques. Some of the dishes, however, incorporate such non-native ingredients as wheat flour and dairy products, and we make no claim that chicken or oatmeal cookies are indigenous American foods.

In this very act of adapting traditional foods and combining them in new ways, the restaurant embodies another fundamental of Native cultures: continual adaptation has been the key to our survival as well as our prosperity. But the foods themselves—whether we call them indigenous or local—remain at the heart of our families and communities.

—KEVIN GOVER (PAWNEE), DIRECTOR
NATIONAL MUSEUM OF THE AMERICAN INDIAN
SMITHSONIAN INSTITUTION

Rev. James O. Arthur (1887–1971). Eating dinner at a Winnebago (Ho-Chunk) camp meeting, August 1913. Winnebago Reservation, Nebraska. N53116

INTRODUCTION

At dawn, I could sense my grandmother's presence in the kitchen. I heard her light steps and deft, efficient movements. She easily pulled open the heavy door on her ancient refrigerator—a feat that took the strength of both my hands—and swiftly snapped it shut as if to keep the chill away. She had an expert way of protecting us from the cold harshness of noise. Morning landed softly at my grandmother's house, wrapped in warmth.

My sisters and I knew her as Lita. She spent many hours preparing meals for us—each one an event. The night before, she would set our places at the table. Big mugs for thick hot chocolate—no two were ever alike. She placed speckled blue plates—the kind used for camping trips—on top of brightly patterned vinyl place mats. The plates welcomed generous helpings of crunchy, seasoned potatoes that she would fry up in a cast-iron skillet. The giant bowl on the table was always full of fresh fruit from the local farm stand. Every day, every night, exploded with flavor at her house. Familiar and novel tastes took their turns dancing with our senses.

Taking full advantage of the fresh produce of California's central coast, Lita took great joy in transforming familiar favorites into new sensations. I remember peeling away a tamale's corn husk to find a soft pillow of moist masa wrapped around the unexpected: sweet whole strawberries! I know my grandmother would have found a kindred spirit in Rich Hetzler, the chef of the Mitsitam Cafe. His Corn and Chocolate Tamales are reminiscent of her spirit of innovation. A marriage of the ancient staple, maize, and legendary chocolate, this dessert is at once a surprise and a comfort.

The combination of chocolate and maize is not new. The people of the land now known as Mexico thickened their chocolate drinks with ground maize, making a thick porridge. They also used hot chiles in the preparation of some of their chocolate drinks, made frothy by transferring them from one vessel to the next. Olmec people first cultivated the cacao tree. Maya people believed that the cacao tree belonged to the gods, and that cacao pods were their gift to humans—a symbol of life and fertility. As such, Maya and Aztec peoples valued cacao beans as a form of currency, and used them in ceremonies. It is common to see images of cacao pods in ancient Mesoamerican architecture and codices, as well as on ceramic vessels, where traces of the drink may still be found.

Maize, which has been integral to the survival of humankind, had its beginnings in central Mexico thousands of years ago. Indigenous farmers through the ages skillfully bred this crop to thrive in diverse conditions, enabling its eventual spread to cover the largest area of any cultivated food on Earth. North American farmers developed a variety of corn that matured in 60 days to accommodate a brief cool season, as well as other varieties that flourished in arid climates. They did the same for beans and squash, the other two crops that, along with corn, constitute what the Haudenosaunee (Iroquois) call the Three Sisters. Corn, beans, and squash are among the greatest gifts bestowed on the world. Their impact on the nutrition and economies of peoples from Europe to Asia cannot be overestimated. To this day, indigenous peoples throughout the Western Hemisphere gather in celebration of corn. The Muscogee gather in July for their Green Corn Ceremonial. They honor the new harvest, praising the Creator and observing a time of atonement. Of the several stomp dances held in northeastern Oklahoma, this is the most widely attended, drawing people of all ages.

Rich Hetzler's ceviche recipe invites me to revisit the many afternoons of my childhood spent at Refugio State Beach. The park is just over the mountains from the Santa Ynez Reservation, where much of my family still resides. We swam, boogie-boarded, looked for sea life, played, and ate. One of our favorite appetizers was, and continues to be, ceviche. Stopping for a snack, we'd take crisp toasted corn tortilla chips and use them to scoop up the translucent fish, which tasted of the ocean. The light, refreshing dish enabled us to continue our activities without feeling too full. All our neighbors along the Pacific Coast, from Mexico to Chile, enjoy many different versions of ceviche, each unique to their regions and communities.

Fish have always been an important part of life for many Native peoples, stimulating economies, good health, and technological ingenuity. Shellfish such as clams, oysters, and quahogs have been enjoyed in abundance by the peoples near bays and inlets. Fish, herring roe, and ocean vegetables like seaweed have nourished coastal peoples for millennia. Those who lived near rivers and lakes developed sophisticated traps for freshwater catch of catfish and trout, to name just a few.

In northern California, the Yurok people welcome the return of chinook and coho salmon twice a year. The salmon comes full circle in this place, from the moment of hatching to its eventual maturity and return home to spawn. The introduction of pesticides and fertilizer on nearby farmlands has resulted in a drastic decline in the salmon population. Most communities along the Pacific Coast share a spiritual, cultural, and economic connection to the salmon, working diligently to protect and honor its sacred cycle, on which more than 137 species of flora and fauna depend.

The ancient technique of roasting salmon on cedar planks (*see page 97*) evokes for me a 1998 gathering in Vancouver, British Columbia, where the Musqueam Nation welcomed people from many First Nations. The salmon our hosts roasted that day was rich and velvety smooth. The freshness was unlike anything I had experienced. The Bannock Bread with Berries (*see page 154*) also reminds me of that feast. Luscious summer berries made a dramatic appearance everywhere, bursting with inky juice, staining our fingers and lips. After we ate, we danced together in friendship, embraced by the warmth of the community house.

This book introduces the peoples, cultures, and histories of the lands we call home. Native American culinary legacy tells a story of who we were, our lives now, and where we are going. The buffalo recipes (*see pages 63, 73, and 106*) remind us of this perennial truth. More than a food source, buffalo were an integral part of cultures on the Great Plains, providing necessary materials for clothes, shelter, and tools. Playing a key role in maintaining environmental balance, buffalo eat the tops of the prairie grasses and move along without depleting the grasslands. The Lakota depended on *wasna* (known also as pemmican), made of dried buffalo meat and chokecherries, to sustain them while hunting. Today, we have learned to value buffalo meat as a lean, iron-rich, and lower-cholesterol alternative to beef.

Wild rice, the seed of a wild water grass, is a healthy food that has been harvested for centuries by the Anishinaabe. On the first day of ricing, they celebrate the harvest with song, dance, and prayer. The Seven Prophecies, also known as the Seven Fires, told the Anishinaabe to move westward until they found food growing on the water. In northern Minnesota, where many Anishinaabe live today, wild rice grows in most of the lakes and rivers. This food is high in fiber, complex carbohydrates, and protein.

The indigenous peoples of Mexico also knew the importance of satisfying, nutritious foods. They grew squash and pumpkins, less for their flesh than for their nutty and versatile seeds, which could be dried and stored easily. The ground seed was used as a flavorful base for thick, delicious sauces. Peanuts, another high-protein food, originated in the Americas and are now used worldwide in a variety of foods and essential products. Chiles are another crop of far-reaching influence in global cuisines, as well as medicine. The word itself is Nahuatl in origin. The Aztec people found relief from toothaches in chiles,

while the Maya people used them to treat asthma, coughs, and sore throats. Today, medical researchers explore the applications of chiles for pain relief.

The flavors in these pages sing to me. When I drink Sugarcane and Mint Agua Fresca, I hear the whisper of palm fronds and the zipperlike sound of the guiro, the gourd instrument musicians have played for generations in the Taino homelands of present-day Cuba and Puerto Rico. Other tastes also speak to me of this culture and place. On a walk in Cuba with Taino elder Don Panchito, he showed me a cacao tree with large green pods. He cracked open the large pod and offered me some of the fleshy pulp inside. The light, refreshing taste was unexpected and rejuvenating. The flavor was unfamiliar, but the warmth of his gesture comforted me, much like my grandmother's cheerful mugs of hot chocolate so many mornings ago.

Inspiration from the far reaches of the hemisphere breathes revelations into these recipes. Voices of those who walked before us rise, telling stories of extraordinary lives. They remind us that the earth has nourished us for millennia. As we continue to reap her many gifts, we must honor and respect her. Each recipe in this book is a journey through our lands and histories, a savory celebration of our legacies. Sit at our table. Share with us. *Mitsitam!*

—NICOLASA I. SANDOVAL
(SANTA YNEZ BAND OF CHUMASH INDIANS)

Tom Jones (Ho-Chunk, b. 1964). View of a feast set up outdoors, 1999. Ho-Chunk, Wisconsin. P28510

Appetizers

Guacamole 10

Arepas with Fresh Tomato Salsa 11

Peruvian Potato Causa 13

Pupusas 15

Ceviche 17

Green Papaya and Sea Bass with Amarillo Vinaigrette 18

Juanita Velasco (Maya) making tortillas as part of a National Museum of the American Indian program about Awal, a corn planting celebration from the highlands of Guatemala, April 2007. © Smithsonian Institution.

GUACAMOLE

Cultivated in Mexico's Tehuacán Valley as early as 6000 BC, avocados were a popular part of the otherwise low-fat Mesoamerican diet. Thirty percent of an avocado's weight comes from oil, and it is the richest in protein of all fruits. The avocado sauce today called guacamole closely resembles its Aztec precursor, which was known to its inventors as *ahuaca-mulli*.

The classic version that follows is flavored with cilantro, onion, chile, and lime juice.

MAKES 2 CUPS

3 avocados, peeled, pitted, and coarsely chopped (reserve 1 pit)
¼ cup minced fresh cilantro
2 tablespoons finely chopped white onion
½ teaspoon seeded and minced serrano chile
   (*see Ingredients and Sources, page 171*)
2 tablespoons fresh lime juice
Salt and freshly ground pepper to taste
Tortilla chips for serving

Put the avocados in a medium bowl and mash with the back of a large slotted spoon. Add the remaining ingredients and stir to mix well. Place the pit in the center of the guacamole (to keep the mixture from discoloring) and serve with tortilla chips for dipping.

Chinantec embroidered cotton woman's huipil (shirt), 1930–1935. Oaxaca State, Mexico. 19/935

Arepas
with Fresh Tomato Salsa

Makes 4 arepas

Fresh Tomato Salsa
    1 tomato, coarsely chopped
    2 scallions, including green parts, coarsely chopped
    ¼ teaspoon seeded and minced ají amarillo, serrano,
        or habanero chile (*see Ingredients and Sources, page 171*)
    4 teaspoons minced fresh cilantro
    1 teaspoon distilled white vinegar
    1 teaspoon corn or canola oil
    Salt to taste

Arepas
    1 cup yellow arepa flour (*see Ingredients and Sources, page 171*)
    1 teaspoon salt
    1¼ cups warm water
    Corn or canola oil for deep-frying

For the salsa: In a blender, combine the tomato, scallions, chile, cilantro, vinegar, and oil and pulse to make a coarse sauce. Stir in the salt and set aside.

For the arepas: In a medium bowl, combine the flour and salt. Stir in the water to make a smooth dough.

In a Dutch oven or large, heavy skillet, heat 3 inches oil to 375°F. Divide the dough into 4 pieces and form each into a cake ¼ to ½ inch thick. Working in batches, if necessary, fry the cakes until golden brown, 2 to 3 minutes. Using a slotted metal spatula, transfer the cakes to a paper towel–lined plate to drain. Keep warm in a low oven. Repeat to cook the remaining dough.

Serve warm, topped with salsa.

Like tortillas and tamales, arepas are one of the original corn breads of the Americas. First prepared by the indigenous peoples of present-day Venezuela and Colombia, arepas remain the basis of a variety of dishes in both countries. In their earliest form, arepas were made from a large-grained, starchy species of maize that was dried and cooked briefly in slaked lime (or wood ashes) and water. The resulting dough was formed into small, flat cakes and cooked either on a special flagstone slab or on a utensil called an aripo, from which the name arepa probably derives.

Arepas of varying thicknesses are today either cooked on a griddle or, as in this recipe, deep-fried—producing a delicious cake that is crisp on the outside and soft within. Here, they are served with a fresh tomato salsa.

Peruvian Potato Causa

PERUVIAN POTATO CAUSA

This molded, layered mashed-potato salad originated in the Andean highlands, where pre-Inka farmers developed hundreds of varieties of potatoes. With Hispanic-influenced modifications, causas have become Peru's national dish. The word *causa* comes from the Quechua *kausay*, meaning "life," or "sustenance of life."

Note: *If purple potatoes are unavailable, an equal amount of Yukon Gold potatoes may be substituted, but the finished salad will not have the layered look that the two different colors provide.*

SERVES 4 TO 6

1 pound unpeeled purple potatoes, scrubbed
    (*see Ingredients and Sources, page 171*)
1 pound unpeeled Yukon Gold potatoes, scrubbed
¼ cup olive oil, plus 1 cup
¼ cup fresh lemon juice
2 teaspoons red or yellow ají limo powder (*see Ingredients and Sources, page 171*) or 1 teaspoon cayenne pepper
2 teaspoons salt
2 cups thinly sliced white onions
½ cup thinly sliced green bell pepper
½ cup thinly sliced red bell pepper
½ cup green olives, pitted and sliced
2 hard-cooked eggs, sliced crosswise

Put the purple and yellow potatoes in separate medium saucepans of salted cold water to cover. Bring to a boil, reduce the heat to a brisk simmer, and cook the potatoes until tender, 15 to 20 minutes. Drain and let cool to the touch. Peel and force the purple potatoes through a ricer into a medium bowl. Clean the ricer; peel and force the yellow potatoes through the ricer into a separate bowl. Alternatively, the potatoes may be peeled then mashed in separate bowls with a potato masher. Add 2 tablespoons of the olive oil, half of the lemon juice, and half of the ají limo or cayenne to each bowl of potatoes. Stir until blended. Season each bowl of potatoes with one teaspoon of salt. Set aside.

In a large pot, combine the 1 cup olive oil, the onions, and green and red bell peppers. Bring to a low simmer over medium-low heat and cook, stirring occasionally, until tender, 40 to 45 minutes. Remove from the heat and let cool.

Line an 8- or 9-inch loaf pan or terrine with plastic wrap. Spoon the purple potato mixture into the pan or terrine and spread into an even layer.

Spread the pepper mixture over the potatoes and top with the olives. Spoon the yellow potato mixture on top and spread into an even layer. Press the potatoes firmly into the pan with your hands or the back of a spoon. Refrigerate for 8 to 10 hours.

Place a plate over the pan or terrine and carefully invert both together to unmold. Remove the plastic wrap and place the egg slices in a row down the center of the terrine. Cut into slices and serve.

Costa Rican Atlantic Watershed (archaeological cultures) stone metate carved in the form of a jaguar, AD 1000–1500. Linea Vieja area, Costa Rica. 23/5780

PUPUSAS

These stuffed corn patties from El Salvador, which are served at pupuserias throughout the Americas, may be filled with meat, beans, cheese, or all three. To make them at home, you will need masa harina, flour made from corn kernels that have been treated with slaked lime and water. This process, first developed by Maya and Aztec cooks, is called nixtamalization, and it greatly increases the protein value of the corn.

For this recipe, the pupusas are filled with cheese and served with a crisp slaw of cabbage and carrots.

MAKES 8 PUPUSAS

Slaw

    2 cups thinly shredded green cabbage
    3 to 4 medium carrots, cut into 2-inch matchsticks (about 1 cup)
    ¼ cup cider vinegar
    ½ cup canola oil
    ½ teaspoon salt

Pupusas

    2 cups masa harina (*see Ingredients and Sources, page 171*)
    1 cup water
    2 teaspoons salt
    1 teaspoon ají amarillo powder (*see Ingredients and Sources, page 171*)
        or 1 teaspoon cayenne pepper
    1 teaspoon red or yellow ají limo powder (*see Ingredients and Sources, page 171*)
    1 cup shredded mozzarella cheese
    3 tablespoons corn or canola oil for frying

For the slaw: In a medium bowl, combine all the ingredients and toss to blend. Let stand at room temperature for 2 to 3 hours.

For the pupusas: In a medium bowl, combine the masa harina and water; stir to make a stiff dough. Stir in the salt and chile powders. Divide into 8 pieces and form each into a disk about 5 inches in diameter. Place 2 tablespoons of cheese in the center of each round. Fold the edges of each round over to cover the cheese. Gently flatten each round into a disk about 3½ inches in diameter.

In a large, heavy skillet, heat the oil over medium-high heat until shimmering. Add the pupusas and cook until golden brown, 4 to 5 minutes on each side. Using a slotted metal spatula, transfer to a paper towel–lined plate to drain.

Place 2 pupusas on 4 small plates and top with the slaw. Serve at once.

Ceviche

CEVICHE

Versions of ceviche, or *cebiche*, are found all along the Pacific Coast from Mexico to Chile, but the technique of "cooking" raw fish or shellfish in acidic fruit juice originated in Peru and Ecuador. The Spanish introduced lemons, limes, and bitter oranges (the fruits most often used for ceviche marinades today) to the Americas in the 1500s, but Inka peoples may have preserved raw seafood in the juice of an indigenous fruit called tumbo long before Europeans arrived. Today, Peruvians often serve their ceviche with pieces of corn on the cob, slices of hard-boiled eggs, slices of sweet potato, and toasted dried corn. Ecuadorans also offer toasted dried corn, along with bowls of popcorn and glasses of the citrus marinade.

SERVES 4

8 cups Court Bouillon (*page 165*)
8 ounces medium shrimp (31 to 35 per pound), shelled and halved lengthwise
8 ounces cleaned calamari, cut into rings
4 cups water
1 tablespoon salt
½ cup thinly sliced red onion
½ cup fresh lime juice
1 tablespoon minced garlic
¼ to ½ teaspoon ají amarillo paste (*see Ingredients and Sources, page 171*) or ¼ teaspoon cayenne pepper
¼ cup minced fresh cilantro
1 teaspoon salt
Freshly ground black pepper to taste

In a large nonreactive pot, bring the Court Bouillon to a simmer. Add the shrimp and calamari, and poach for 1 minute. Using a slotted spoon, transfer seafood to a cold-water bath for 1 minute to stop the cooking. Transfer to a paper towel–lined plate to drain.

In a medium bowl, combine the water and salt; stir to dissolve the salt. Add the onion and let soak for 10 minutes; drain.

In a medium bowl, combine the calamari, shrimp, and ¼ cup of the lime juice. Let stand for 1 hour. Drain, discarding the lime juice. Add the onion slices, garlic, ají amarillo paste or cayenne, cilantro, and the remaining lime juice. Toss to blend. Season with the salt and pepper. Cover and refrigerate for at least 30 minutes or up to 2 hours.

Divide among 4 bowls and serve.

Green Papaya and Sea Bass
with Amarillo Vinaigrette

Papayas are one of the many tropical fruits first documented by Spanish explorers in southern Mesoamerica. Juan Díaz, the chaplain for an expedition led by Juan de Grijalva in 1518, described "peaches" on the island of Cozumel off the coast of Yucatán that weighed more than three pounds. He could well have been referring to papayas.

In this recipe, pickled green papaya, onion, and sweet peppers are tossed with a spicy vinaigrette and served as a bed for sea bass that has been "cooked" like ceviche in the pickling liquid.

Serves 4 to 6

Pickled Green Papaya
    1 cup cider vinegar
    ½ cup honey
    2 cups water
    1 cup fresh lime juice
    2 teaspoons seeded and minced serrano chile
        (*see Ingredients and Sources, page 171*)
    1 cup chopped fresh cilantro
    1 teaspoon peppercorns
    1 clove
    1 bay leaf
    1½ tablespoons red pepper flakes
    2 cinnamon sticks
    1 green papaya, peeled, seeded, and cut into strips 1 inch wide and 2½ inches long, about 2 cups (*see Ingredients and Sources, page 171*)
    ¼ cup red onion cut into 2-inch matchsticks
    ¼ cup red bell pepper cut into 2-inch matchsticks
    ¼ cup green bell pepper cut into 2-inch matchsticks

Amarillo Vinaigrette
    2 tablespoons ají amarillo paste (*see Ingredients and Sources, page 171*)
    ¼ cup fresh lemon juice
    2 tablespoons honey
    ¾ cup canola oil

Sea Bass
    1 pound sea bass or other white-fleshed fish fillets, cut into strips ¼ inch thick and 3 inches wide
    ¼ cup minced fresh cilantro

For the pickled green papaya: In a medium nonreactive pot, combine all the ingredients except the papaya and stir to blend. Bring to a boil over high heat and cook for 10 minutes. Remove from the heat and let cool. Add the papaya and let stand at room temperature for at least 24 hours or up to 36 hours. Strain the papaya, reserving the liquid. Put the pickled papaya in a medium bowl and add the onion and red and green bell peppers.

For the vinaigrette: In a medium bowl, combine the ají amarillo paste, lemon juice, and honey. Gradually whisk in the oil until incorporated. Add the vinaigrette to the papaya mixture and toss to coat.

For the sea bass: Put the sea bass and cilantro in the reserved pickling liquid and let stand for 20 minutes; drain.

To serve, transfer the papaya mixture to a serving plate or shallow bowl and top with the sea bass.

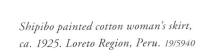

Shipibo painted cotton woman's skirt, ca. 1925. Loreto Region, Peru. 19/5940

Soups

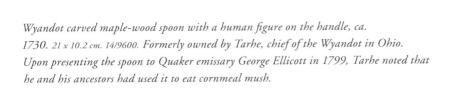

Wyandot carved maple-wood spoon with a human figure on the handle, ca. 1730. 21 x 10.2 cm. 14/9600. Formerly owned by Tarhe, chief of the Wyandot in Ohio. Upon presenting the spoon to Quaker emissary George Ellicott in 1799, Tarhe noted that he and his ancestors had used it to eat cornmeal mush.

Ales Hrdlicka (1869–1943). An Akimel O'odham (Pima) woman grinds corn on a metate, with two children nearby, 1898–1902. Arizona. P04955

SQUASH BLOSSOM SOUP

Squash and their blossoms are used in Native cooking wherever the vegetables are grown. For Pueblo peoples the flowers have spiritual meaning. As one of the plant *katsinas*, or spirits, who appear in the form of masked dancers during Hopi and Zuni ceremonies, the Squash Katsina, or Patung, brings health, fertility, and long life.

This version of squash blossom soup is a rich blend of beans and vegetables, including two kinds of squash, with a garnish of zucchini blossoms.

Paul J. Woolf (1899–1985). Diné (Navajo) woman gathering squash, ca. 1940. Ramah Navajo Reservation, New Mexico. P24080A

SERVES 4 TO 6

2 tablespoons olive oil
½ cup diced yellow onion
¼ cup diced leek (white part only)
1 tablespoon minced garlic
½ cup diced carrot
½ cup diced green bell pepper
½ cup diced red bell pepper
½ cup diced Yukon Gold potato
1 bay leaf
2 cups diced yellow summer squash
10 to 12 small pattypan (scalloped) squash, halved horizontally
4 cups homemade vegetable stock (*page 165*) or canned low-sodium vegetable stock
1 teaspoon powdered saffron
½ cup cooked pinto beans (*page 167*), drained, or canned pinto beans, drained and rinsed
½ cup diced tomato
Leaves from 1 fresh marjoram sprig, minced
Leaves from 2 fresh flat-leaf parsley sprigs, minced
¼ cup fresh lemon juice
Salt and freshly ground pepper to taste
4 to 6 zucchini blossoms for garnish (*see Ingredients and Sources, page 171*)

In a large saucepan, heat the olive oil over medium heat and sauté the onion, leek, and garlic until the onion and leek are translucent, about 3 minutes. Add the carrot, green and red bell pepper, potato, and bay leaf. Sauté for 3 or 4 minutes. Add three-fourths of the summer squash and three-fourths of the pattypan squash. Sauté for 5 minutes.

Add the stock and saffron; bring to a simmer. Add the remaining squash (both kinds) and the pinto beans. Cook for 15 minutes, or until all the vegetables are tender. Stir in the diced tomato, herbs, and lemon juice. Season with salt and pepper, and remove the bay leaf. Garnish each serving with a zucchini blossom.

Probably Chimú (archaeological culture) pottery bottle in the form of a squash, AD *1200–1400. Lambayeque region, Peru.*

28 x 15.5 cm. 15/1457

BUTTERNUT SQUASH SOUP

One of the Americas' oldest cultivated crops, squashes were, and still are, a staple for Native people, with different species flourishing in nearly every part of the Americas. In northern regions, most of a community's harvest was cut into strips, dried for several days, and stored for months. Ojibwe cooks in the Great Lakes region might have reconstituted dried squash or pumpkin by boiling it with game, or with maple sugar.

This soup is also flavored with maple, but it incorporates butter, cream, and spices in a hearty post-Contact version.

Note: *The soup improves in flavor if made 1 day ahead. Let cool, then cover and refrigerate. Reheat over medium-low heat, stirring occasionally.*

SERVES 4 TO 6

6 tablespoons unsalted butter
1½ pounds butternut squash, peeled, seeded, and cut into 1-inch cubes (about 3 cups)
½ yellow onion, chopped
3 stalks celery, chopped
1 carrot, peeled and chopped
3 cups homemade vegetable stock (*page 165*) or canned low-sodium vegetable stock
Spice sachet: 1 bay leaf, 2 allspice berries, 1 clove, and 1 small cinnamon stick, tied in a cheesecloth square or placed in a wire mesh tea filter
1 cup heavy cream
2 teaspoons salt
Freshly ground pepper to taste
2 tablespoons maple syrup

In a large saucepan, melt 2 tablespoons of the butter over medium-low heat. Add the squash, onion, celery, and carrot, and sauté until the squash is tender, about 30 minutes. Add the stock and spice sachet. Bring to a simmer and cook for 30 to 40 minutes, or until flavorful.

Remove the sachet. In batches, puree the soup in a blender. Return to the pan and add the cream. Reheat over low heat. Season with the salt and pepper. Stir in the remaining ¼ cup butter and the maple syrup.

Tortilla Soup

Tortilla Soup

Thin, flat, round cakes made from nixtamalized maize (field corn softened in a mixture of slaked lime and water) are one of the original mainstays of Mesoamerican cooking. In this soup, they are used to thicken a mixture of vegetables and chicken stock, recalling the maize-thickened drinks on which Maya and Aztec diets were based.

This recipe may be easily doubled.

Serves 4 to 6 as a first course

2 tablespoons corn or canola oil
½ small yellow onion, chopped
4 large cloves garlic, minced
½ zucchini, chopped
1 yellow summer squash, chopped
½ small red bell pepper, chopped
½ small yellow bell pepper, chopped
10 plum (Roma) tomatoes, chopped
4 cups chicken stock
4 corn tortillas
2 tablespoons minced fresh epazote
 (*see Ingredients and Sources, page 171*) or cilantro
Salt and freshly ground pepper to taste
Sour cream for garnish

In a large soup pot, heat the oil over medium heat and sauté the onion, garlic, zucchini, squash, red and yellow bell peppers, and tomatoes for 10 to 15 minutes, or until tender. Add the stock and bring to a simmer. Cook for 15 minutes. Set aside for about 10 minutes to cool slightly.

Meanwhile, preheat the oven to 350°F. Put the tortillas on a baking sheet and bake for 10 to 15 minutes, or until crisp and beginning to brown. Remove from the oven and break into large pieces.

Working in batches, puree the soup and tortillas in a blender or food processor. Return to the pan to reheat. Stir in the epazote or cilantro. Season with salt and pepper. Garnish each serving with a dollop of sour cream.

PEANUT SOUP

Peanuts are native to South America but had arrived as far north as Mexico by AD 500. In the 1500s, the Portuguese brought peanuts, along with maize and sweet potatoes, to West Africa from Brazil. The legume was later introduced to the United States from Africa. There is archaeological evidence that in Peru around 3000 BC, peanuts were eaten roasted in the shell, just as they are in baseball stadiums today.

2 tablespoons canola oil
½ cup chopped yellow onion
1 serrano chile, seeded and coarsely chopped
    (*see Ingredients and Sources, page 171*)
2 cups unsalted dry-roasted peanuts
4 cups chicken stock, plus more as needed
½ cup heavy cream
½ cup (1 stick) unsalted butter
1 teaspoon cayenne pepper
2 tablespoons fresh lime juice
Salt to taste
Fresh cilantro leaves for garnish

In a large, heavy saucepan, heat the oil over medium heat and sauté the onion and serrano chile until the onion is translucent, about 3 minutes. Stir in the peanuts and cook, stirring occasionally, until their oil is released, about 30 minutes. Stir in the 2 cups chicken stock, bring just to a boil, and simmer over medium heat until the peanuts are tender, 20 to 25 minutes.

In a blender, puree the soup in batches until smooth. Return to the pan and place over low heat. Add the cream and butter and stir until the butter is melted. Add more chicken stock to thin the soup, if you wish, unless using for Chicken Tamales (*page 92*). Stir in the cayenne, lime juice, and salt. Taste and adjust the seasoning. Garnish each serving with cilantro.

SMOKED PORK AND QUINOA SOUP

Versions of this soup—without the pork—date to the time of the Inka Empire. Quinoa, cultivated for thousands of years in the Andes, was so fundamental to Inka people that they called it *chesiya mama*, the Mother Grain. At solstice celebrations, priests offered vessels filled with quinoa to Inti, the Sun. The leaves of this plant are highly nutritious, while the seeds, which have become widely available in North America, yield more protein than any other grain. Cooked with a ham hock, chicken stock, and mustard greens, they make a hearty main-course soup.

Note: *Dandelion greens, beet greens, or kale may be substituted for the mustard greens.*

SERVES 4 TO 6

3 tablespoons unsalted butter
1 carrot, peeled and diced
½ cup diced yellow onion
1 cup diced celery
½ teaspoon red pepper flakes
2 tablespoons minced garlic
7 cups chicken stock
1 smoked ham hock
½ cup red quinoa, rinsed (*see Ingredients and Sources, page 171*)
½ cup black quinoa, rinsed (*see Ingredients and Sources, page 171*)
1 pound mustard greens, well rinsed and center rib removed, chopped (2 packed cups), or 10 ounces frozen mustard greens (*see Ingredients and Sources, page 171*)
Salt and freshly ground pepper to taste
3 tablespoons minced fresh chervil

In a large soup pot, melt the butter over medium heat and sauté the carrot, onion, celery, and red pepper flakes until the onion is translucent, about 3 minutes. Stir in the garlic and cook for 1 minute. Add the stock and ham hock. Bring to a boil, reduce the heat to a simmer, and cook for 30 minutes. Add the quinoa (both kinds), cover, and cook for 30 minutes, or until the quinoa is translucent and tender.

Remove from the heat and remove the ham hock. Let the ham hock cool to the touch, then remove the meat from the bone and return the meat to the hot broth. Stir the mustard greens into the pot until wilted. Season with salt and pepper. Garnish each serving with some of the minced chervil.

QUAHOG CHOWDER

The shells of the northern quahog—a clam species whose original habitat extended from New Jersey to Maine—were the source of many of the small, cylindrical beads called wampum. Northeast Native peoples and European diplomats used belts woven from the beads to seal treaties, record events, or communicate special messages. Since quahogs with purple or purple-edged shells were harder to find and more difficult to work than the more common white-shelled variety, purple wampum beads were considered more valuable than their white counterparts.

In this chowder, clams are cooked with corn kernels and the fresh cobs for a sweet depth of flavor.

Edward S. Curtis (1868–1952). The Clam Digger, ca. 1900. A Suquamish woman digging for clams. Puget Sound, Washington. P11177

SERVES 4 TO 6

4 ears corn, husked
4 cups Court Bouillon (*page 165*)
10 to 12 large clams, such as quahogs or top necks, scrubbed
¼ cup unsalted butter
½ cup diced yellow onion
½ cup diced green bell pepper
¼ cup diced celery
2 tablespoons minced garlic
1 teaspoon freshly ground black pepper
¼ cup all-purpose flour
1 bay leaf
1 cup peeled, diced russet potato
¼ cup heavy cream
Salt, freshly ground black pepper, and cayenne pepper to taste

Cut the kernels from the ears of corn and set aside, reserving the cobs. In a stockpot, bring the Court Bouillon to a low simmer and add the clams. Cook for 4 to 5 minutes, or until the clams open. Using a slotted spoon, remove the clams from the bouillon and set aside. Reserve the bouillon. Discard any clams that do not open. Remove the clams from their shells and cut the meat into bite-sized pieces if they are large. Set the clams aside.

In a large pot, melt the butter over medium heat and sauté the onion, bell pepper, celery, garlic, and black pepper until the onion is translucent, about 3 minutes. Add the flour and cook, stirring constantly, for 5 minutes. Add the bay leaf. Gradually whisk in all but ½ cup of the reserved Court Bouillon and bring to a boil, stirring frequently, until thickened. Reduce the heat to a simmer and add half of the corn kernels and all the reserved corncobs. In a blender, puree the remaining corn kernels with the ½ cup reserved Court Bouillon and add to the pot. Add the potato and simmer for 10 to 15 minutes, or until the corn is tender. Add the clams and cream. Simmer for 15 minutes more. Remove the corncobs and bay leaf. Season the soup with salt, pepper, and cayenne.

Salads

Three Sisters Salad 35
Celery Root Salad 37
Fiddlehead Fern Salad 39
Green Mango Salad 40
Fennel Salad with Fig Vinaigrette 41
Cabbage Salad with Spiced Peanuts and Pineapple 42
Seaweed and Wild Mushroom Salad 45
Peruvian Potato Salad 46
Roasted Sunchoke Salad with Ginger Vinaigrette 47
Root Vegetables with Mustard Seed Vinaigrette 49
Wild Rice Salad 51
Black Bean and Roasted Corn Salad 52
Quinoa Salad 53
Hominy Salad with Saffron Vinaigrette 54
Smoked Trout and Watercress Salad 55
Smoked Duck Salad 57

A Maya fruit and vegetable market, ca. 1960. Guatemala. P28489

Three Sisters Salad

THREE SISTERS SALAD

In Haudenosaunee (Iroquois) villages, as in many other Native communities, women planted, hoed, weeded, and harvested communally, often working in large groups. The staple crops they grew—corn, beans, and squash—came to be known as The Three Sisters. Not only do the three foods grow well together (the beans climb the natural trellis provided by the cornstalks, while the broad-leaved squash plants spread out below, preventing weeds and keeping moisture in the soil), but when cooked together they provide nearly complete nutrition.

Here, grilled squash and corn are mixed with cranberry beans and yellow and red tomatoes.

SERVES 4 TO 6

Apple Cider Vinaigrette
6 tablespoons apple cider vinegar
¼ cup honey
¾ cup canola oil
Salt and freshly ground pepper to taste

Salad
2 zucchini, halved lengthwise and seeded
2 yellow summer squash, halved lengthwise and seeded
2 ears corn, husked
¼ cup canola oil
Salt and freshly ground pepper to taste
2 cups cooked cranberry beans (*page 166*), drained
1 medium yellow tomato or ¾ cup yellow cherry tomatoes, diced
2 plum (Roma) tomatoes or ¾ cup cherry tomatoes, diced

For the vinaigrette: In a small bowl, combine all the ingredients and whisk to blend. Cover and refrigerate for at least 1 hour, or up to 10 days.

For the salad: Prepare a hot fire in a charcoal grill, or preheat a gas grill to high. Brush the zucchini, squash, and corn with oil. Season the vegetables on all sides with salt and pepper. Grill the zucchini and squash until crisp-tender and grill-marked on both sides, about 10 minutes. At the same time, grill the corn until lightly browned, turning to cook all sides, 4 to 5 minutes.

Transfer the zucchini and squash to a cutting board and finely dice, then empty into a large bowl. Cut the kernels from the corn and add to the bowl along with the beans and the yellow and red tomatoes. Add ¼ cup vinaigrette and toss to coat. Season with salt and pepper and toss again. Serve at room temperature or cold.

CELERY ROOT SALAD

Edible roots—along with salmon, venison, and berries—are one of the four sacred foods for many communities along the North Pacific Coast. With forests abundantly supplied with wild plants and oceans teeming with fish and shellfish, these communities were able to sustain themselves for thousands of years without cultivated crops. A transplant from Europe, celery root, or celeriac, has grown wild in North America for centuries.

Odowa (Ottawa) maple-wood feast bowl with two handles, one representing an animal's head, ca. 1880. Michigan. 16/9037

SERVES 4 TO 6

Dressing
   ½ cup mayonnaise
   ½ cup sour cream
   2 tablespoons Dijon mustard
   2 tablespoons fresh lemon juice
   Salt and freshly ground pepper to taste

Salad
   1 celery root (celeriac), peeled
      and cut into 2-inch matchsticks
      (see Ingredients and Sources, page 171)
   1 cup red radishes cut into 2-inch matchsticks
   ½ cup chopped scallions, including some
      of the green parts

For the dressing: In a small bowl, combine the mayonnaise, sour cream, mustard, and lemon juice. Stir to blend. Season with salt and pepper.

For the salad: In a medium bowl, combine the celery root, radishes, and scallions. Add the dressing to the vegetables. Toss to blend. Cover and refrigerate for 2 to 4 hours.

Fiddlehead Fern Salad

FIDDLEHEAD FERN SALAD

In communities along the North Pacific Coast, fern roots were a valuable source of starch. The roots were baked in embers, then eaten immediately or dried and ground into flour for use in the winter. Fiddleheads are young, curled fern shoots that grow in forested areas of the North Pacific and North Atlantic coasts. Some Native cooks toss boiled fiddleheads in strongly flavored oolichan, or candlefish, oil.

The ferns are available fresh in gourmet markets for only a short period in the spring, any time from April to July, depending on the region. Their fresh green taste is complemented by the smoky flavor of bacon in this salad.

SERVES 4 TO 6

Apple Cider Vinaigrette
6 tablespoons apple cider vinegar
¼ cup honey
¾ cup canola oil
Salt and freshly ground pepper to taste

Salad
3 to 4 slices bacon
1 pound fiddlehead ferns
2 cups radishes, coarsely chopped
1 cup coarsely chopped seedless cucumber
½ cup minced fresh chives
Salt and freshly ground pepper to taste

For the vinaigrette: In a small bowl, combine all the ingredients and whisk to blend. Cover and refrigerate for at least 1 hour, or up to 10 days.

For the salad: In a medium skillet, fry the bacon over medium heat until crisp. Using tongs, transfer to a paper towel–lined plate to drain. Crumble the bacon and set aside.

In a pot of salted boiling water, blanch the ferns for 2 minutes. Transfer to a bowl of ice water to cool. Drain and transfer to a salad bowl. Add the radishes, cucumber, and chives to the ferns. Add ½ cup vinaigrette and toss to coat. Season with salt and pepper. Top each serving with crumbled bacon.

Green Mango Salad

Mangoes are cultivated in Florida, Mesoamerica, and South America and come in many sizes and colors. Green (unripe) mangoes are sometimes prepared as a vegetable or, as in this recipe, pickled. Here, they are combined with a brilliant red puree of prickly pear cactus, which grows wild in the southern areas of present-day Arizona and New Mexico and has been a part of the local Native diet for centuries. Spiny, disc-like "pads" called nopales form the body of the plant, producing flowers that mature into prickly, dark red fruits in late summer. For the Tohono O'odham of southern Arizona, the word for *purple* stems from *'i:bhai*, meaning "prickly pear." Note that Diné (Navajo) weavers have used the fruit as a dye, and be aware that the puree can easily stain clothing and cooking surfaces.

Pickled Mangoes
    1 cup distilled white vinegar
    ¼ cup honey
    1 cup water
    3 tablespoons fresh lime juice
    ¼ cup coarsely chopped fresh cilantro
    1 teaspoon black peppercorns
    3 cloves
    4 bay leaves
    2 tablespoons red pepper flakes
    1 cinnamon stick
    3 green mangoes, peeled, pitted, and cut into pieces
        ½ inch wide and 2 inches long (*see Ingredients and Sources, page 171*)

Salad
    1 cup prickly pear puree (*see Ingredients and Sources, page 171*)
    2 red bell peppers, cut into 2-inch matchsticks
    ½ red onion cut into 2-inch matchsticks
    ¼ cup fresh cilantro leaves

For the pickled mangoes: In a large nonreactive pot, combine all the pickling liquid ingredients and bring to a boil. Remove from the heat.

Put the mango pieces in a large bowl and pour the pickling liquid over. Refrigerate for at least 18 hours, or up to 24 hours. Drain the mangoes and set aside.

For the salad: In a small saucepan, bring the prickly pear puree to a simmer over medium-low heat. Cook until reduced by half, about 10 minutes. In a large bowl, combine the mangoes, bell peppers, onion, and cilantro. Toss with the prickly pear reduction.

FENNEL SALAD
WITH FIG VINAIGRETTE

Roasted fennel, combined with thin, crunchy slices of asparagus, parsnip, and carrot, makes a refreshing salad when dressed with a vinaigrette of dried figs and honey. At the Mitsitam Cafe, this salad is served with Cedar-Planked Fire-Roasted Salmon (*page 97*).

SERVES 4 TO 6

Fig Vinaigrette
⅓ cup sherry or cider vinegar
¼ cup dried figs
¾ cup canola oil
¼ cup honey
Salt and freshly ground pepper to taste

Salad
1 fennel bulb, trimmed, halved lengthwise,
    and cut into thin lengthwise strips (reserve fronds)
3 to 4 tablespoons canola oil
2 to 3 carrots, peeled and cut into 2-inch matchsticks
2 to 3 parsnips, peeled and cut into 2-inch matchsticks
6 to 8 thick asparagus stalks, trimmed, bases peeled,
    and cut into long shavings with a vegetable peeler (1 cup)
Salt and freshly ground pepper to taste

For the vinaigrette: In a small, heavy saucepan, cook the vinegar over low heat to reduce by half. Put the figs in a small bowl and pour the hot vinegar over; let stand for 10 to 15 minutes to plump. Using a slotted spoon, transfer the figs to a cutting board and cut them into quarters. Whisk the oil, then the honey into the vinegar. Season with salt and pepper. Return the figs to the vinaigrette.

For the salad: Preheat the oven to 350°F. In a small baking pan, toss the fennel with the oil to coat. Roast for 15 to 20 minutes, or until tender. Remove from the oven and let cool.

In a medium bowl, combine the fennel, carrots, parsnips, and asparagus. Add the vinaigrette and lightly toss to coat. Season with salt and pepper. Mince some of the reserved fennel fronds, and sprinkle them over the salad.

CABBAGE SALAD
WITH SPICED PEANUTS AND PINEAPPLE

Pineapples originated in the lowlands of Brazil, where several species still grow wild. Cultivation had spread at least to the Caribbean by the time Columbus "discovered" the fruit in 1493. One of the most immediately popular of all the foods introduced to Europe in the 1500s, the fruit was soon being grown in tropical regions worldwide, although it did not reach Hawai'i until 1777. The word for "pineapple" in most languages is descended from its Brazilian Tupí name: *nana* or *anana*.

The pineapple's sweetness is complemented here by crunchy cabbage, peanuts toasted with chili powder and cayenne, and a tamarind vinaigrette.

SERVES 4 TO 6

Tamarind Vinaigrette
¼ cup tamarind pulp (*see Ingredients and Sources, page 171*)
¼ cup rice wine vinegar
¼ cup honey
½ cup canola oil
Salt and freshly ground pepper to taste

Spiced Peanuts
⅓ cup unsalted dry-roasted peanuts
1 teaspoon water
1 tablespoon chili powder
¼ teaspoon cayenne pepper
1 tablespoon sweet Hungarian paprika
1 teaspoon salt
1 teaspoon freshly ground pepper

Salad
¼ head green cabbage, cored and cut crosswise
    into 1-inch-wide slices
¼ head red cabbage, cored and cut crosswise
    into 1-inch-wide slices
¼ cup carrot cut into 2-inch matchsticks
1 cup cubed fresh pineapple
½ thinly sliced red onion
½ cup chopped scallions, including some of the green parts
½ cup fresh cilantro leaves

For the vinaigrette: In a small bowl, combine the tamarind pulp, vinegar, and honey. Gradually whisk in the oil until incorporated. Add salt and pepper to taste. Cover and store in the refrigerator for up to 1 week.

For the peanuts: Preheat the oven to 350°F. Put the peanuts in a small bowl and sprinkle with water. Add the spices, salt, and pepper and toss to coat. Sift peanuts from spice and spread on a rimmed baking sheet. Roast in the oven until lightly toasted and fragrant, 5 to 8 minutes. Remove from the oven, pour into a bowl, and let cool.

For the salad: In a medium bowl, combine the two kinds of cabbage, the carrot, pineapple, red onion, scallions, and spiced peanuts. Toss to mix. Add ½ cup vinaigrette and toss to coat. Add the cilantro and toss once more to blend.

SEAWEED AND WILD MUSHROOM SALAD

SERVES 4 TO 6

Spicy Vinaigrette
 1/4 cup rice wine vinegar
1 tablespoon honey
1 1/2 teaspoons red pepper flakes
1 1/2 teaspoons minced garlic
1/2 teaspoon ají panco paste (*see Ingredients and Sources, page 171*)
 or more red pepper flakes to taste
1/2 cup canola oil

Salad
1 cup dried wakame seaweed (*see Ingredients and Sources, page 171*)
1 bunch hen-of-the-woods (maitake) mushrooms, or 6 to 8 shiitake
 mushrooms, stemmed (*see Ingredients and Sources, page 171*)
6 to 8 cremini mushrooms, halved
6 to 8 button mushrooms, halved
1/4 cup canola oil
Salt and freshly ground pepper to taste

For the vinaigrette: In a small bowl, combine the vinegar, honey, red pepper flakes, garlic, and ají panco. Gradually whisk in the oil until incorporated.

For the salad: Preheat the oven to 450°F. Soak the seaweed in lukewarm water to cover for 10 to 15 minutes. Drain, pat dry, and set aside.

In a small bowl, toss the mushrooms with the oil, salt, and pepper. Spread the mushrooms on a rimmed baking sheet and roast in the oven for 5 to 10 minutes, or until soft. Remove from the oven and let cool.

In a medium bowl, combine the seaweed and mushrooms. Add the vinaigrette and toss to coat. Taste and adjust the seasoning.

Many species of seaweed and kelp supplemented the fish-based diet of communities along the North Pacific Coast. Harvested at low tide and dried, seaweed can be eaten as a protein-rich snack or added to soups and stews. Layers of fresh seaweed also cover fish and other foods as they steam in a pit-cooking technique that is common to many coastal Native cultures.

The ocean flavor of the seaweed is balanced in this salad with the woodsy taste of roasted mushrooms and a spicy vinaigrette.

Edward S. Curtis (1868–1952). Gathering Seaweed—Clayaquot, ca. 1910. Two Tla-o-qui-aht (Clayaquot) women collecting seaweed. Probably Vancouver Island. Courtesy of the Library of Congress.

Peruvian Potato Salad

Pre-Inka peoples in the highlands of Peru domesticated potatoes between 3700 and 3000 BC. Even today, Peruvian markets display potatoes in dozens of colors, sizes, and flavors unknown in North America. Although Inka conquerors tended to favor maize, and other crops traveled around the world more swiftly after the Spanish "discovered" them in the 1500s, potatoes eventually became essential to peasant diets in Ireland, Russia, and northern and central Europe.

In this salad, purple potatoes add their dramatic color to a mixture of white and yellow potatoes and a vibrant saffron-yellow dressing.

Serves 4 to 6

Dressing
1 cup (8 ounces) cream cheese at room temperature
2 tablespoons ground turmeric
1 cup sour cream
¼ cup fresh lemon juice
¼ cup heavy cream
Salt and freshly ground pepper to taste

Salad
4 to 6 unpeeled purple or red potatoes, cut into 1½-inch cubes
   (*see Ingredients and Sources, page 171*)
8 to 10 unpeeled red potatoes, cut into 1½-inch cubes
3 to 4 unpeeled Yukon Gold potatoes, cut into 1½-inch cubes
¼ cup olive oil
Salt and freshly ground pepper to taste
¼ cup green olives, pitted and sliced
¼ cup black olives, pitted and sliced
3 tablespoons chopped scallions, including some green parts
¼ cup finely diced red onion
2 hard-cooked eggs, chopped

For the dressing: Combine all the ingredients in a blender or food processor and puree until smooth. Cover and refrigerate until ready to serve.

For the salad: In a covered steamer over simmering water, steam the three kinds of potatoes until tender, 25 to 30 minutes. Remove from the steamer and let cool.

Put the potatoes in a serving bowl. Add the oil, salt, and pepper and toss to coat. Spoon the dressing over the top and sprinkle with the green and black olives, scallions, red onion, and hard-cooked eggs.

Roasted Sunchoke Salad
with Ginger Vinaigrette

Native to North America, the sunchoke is a tuber with a mild flavor similar to that of new potatoes or chestnuts. In many Native communities, sunchokes, which grow from the roots of a sunflower species, are dug up in fall, after the first frost, and eaten raw or cooked like a potato. Cherokee cooks make sunchoke (*gv ge* in the Cherokee language) pickles and preserves.

For this salad, sunchokes are roasted and tossed with dried berries and sunflower seeds, then dressed with a sweet and tangy ginger vinaigrette.

Serves 4 to 6

Ginger Vinaigrette
  2 tablespoons rice wine vinegar
  1 tablespoon honey
  1 tablespoon grated fresh ginger
  ¼ teaspoon minced garlic
  ½ cup canola oil

Salad
  1 pound unpeeled sunchokes (also known as Jerusalem
      artichokes) (*see Ingredients and Sources, page 171*),
      scrubbed and cut into bite-sized pieces
  ¼ cup canola oil
  Salt and freshly ground pepper to taste
  ¼ cup dried blueberries or currants
  ½ cup toasted, cooled sunflower seeds (*page 167*)
  ½ cup finely shredded arugula
  ½ cup frisée lettuce leaves

For the vinaigrette: In a small bowl, whisk the vinegar, honey, ginger, and garlic together. Gradually whisk in the oil.

For the salad: Preheat the oven to 400°F. Put the sunchokes in a medium bowl and toss with the oil, salt, and pepper. Spread on a rimmed baking sheet and roast until crisp-tender, about 10 minutes. Remove from the oven and let cool.

In a large bowl, combine the sunchokes, blueberries or currants, sunflower seeds, arugula, and frisée. Add the vinaigrette and toss to coat. Taste and adjust the seasoning.

Root Vegetables
with Mustard Seed Vinaigrette

This winter salad mixes a variety of crisp roasted vegetables with a honey-mustard dressing.

Serves 4 to 6

Mustard Seed Vinaigrette
    3 tablespoons cider vinegar
    2 tablespoons honey
    1½ tablespoons whole-grain mustard
    ½ cup canola oil
    Salt and freshly ground pepper to taste
    2 tablespoons black or yellow mustard seeds
       (*see Ingredients and Sources, page 171*)

Salad
    3 to 4 carrots, peeled and cut into 1-inch cubes
    2 to 3 parsnips, peeled and cut into 1-inch cubes
    2 red potatoes, peeled and cut into 1-inch cubes
    2 turnips, peeled and cut into 1-inch cubes
    1 to 2 golden beets, peeled and cut into 1-inch cubes
    ¼ cup canola oil
    Salt and freshly ground pepper to taste

For the vinaigrette: In a medium bowl, combine the vinegar, honey, and mustard. Gradually whisk in the oil until incorporated. Stir in the salt, pepper, and mustard seeds. Cover and refrigerate.

For the salad: Preheat the oven to 350°F. Put the vegetables in a medium bowl and toss with the oil, salt, and pepper. Spread on a rimmed baking sheet and roast until crisp-tender, 50 minutes to 1 hour. Remove from the oven and let cool slightly.

Transfer the roasted vegetables to a medium bowl and add the vinaigrette. Toss to coat. Taste and adjust the seasoning.

Almira Buffalo Bone Jackson (Assiniboine, 1917–2004), Sunny Spring Day, *1968–1988. Pieced cotton quilt with a central star motif surrounded by a border of half-stars. Wolf Point, Fort Peck Reservation, Montana. 26/6319*

With the near disappearance of the buffalo in the late 1800s, women in Plains communities began making cloth quilts as a ritual and practical replacement for robes made of bison hide. They incorporated into the quilts many of the patterns and motifs that had been painted on the hide robes, including various star patterns.

Wild Rice Salad

WILD RICE SALAD

Apple Cider Vinaigrette
    6 tablespoons apple cider vinegar
    ¼ cup honey
    ¾ cup canola oil
    Salt and freshly ground pepper to taste

Salad
    6 cups homemade vegetable stock (*page 165*)
        or canned low-sodium chicken broth
    1½ cups wild rice
    1 carrot, peeled and cut into 2-inch matchsticks
    3 tablespoons dried cranberries
    1 plum (Roma) tomato, finely diced
    4 to 5 scallions, including some green parts, finely chopped
    ½ cup pine nuts, toasted and cooled (*page 167*)
    ¼ cup unsalted raw pumpkin seeds, toasted and cooled (*page 167*)
    3 bunches watercress, stemmed

Wild rice flourishes in hundreds of shallow lakes and waterways surrounding the North American Great Lakes. The traditional Ojibwe method of harvesting wild rice was to pole a canoe through the rice field and gently knock the kernels off the tops of the grassy plant into the bottom of the boat. Back at the rice camp, the kernels would be parched in a kettle over a slow fire to dry completely. Then, men and boys wearing clean moccasins would dance on the rice to remove the outer hulls. Finally, women would winnow the kernels by tossing them in a large birch bark basket, using the wind to loosen the last fragments of hull. Today, Ojibwe families on the White Earth Reservation in Minnesota still harvest wild rice in canoes, but they process the kernels in mechanized mills.

In this salad, the cooked rice is blended with pine nuts, pumpkin seeds, and dried cranberries and served on a bed of watercress.

For the vinaigrette: In a small bowl, combine all the ingredients and whisk to blend. Cover and refrigerate for at least 1 hour, or up to 10 days.

For the salad: In a large saucepan, combine the stock and wild rice. Bring to a boil, then reduce the heat to a simmer. Cover and cook until tender, 45 to 55 minutes. Spread the rice on a baking sheet and let cool.

Scrape the rice into a large bowl and add the carrot, dried cranberries, tomato, scallions, pine nuts, and pumpkin seeds. Toss to mix. Add ½ cup vinaigrette and toss to coat. Cover and refrigerate for at least 1 hour. Salad may be served chilled or brought up to room temperature. To serve, divide the watercress among salad plates and top with the wild rice salad.

Black Bean and Roasted Corn Salad

The combination of beans and corn—developed and refined in Mesoamerica and South America during the approximately 6,000 years before Europeans arrived—can provide all the protein requirements for most human adults. Black beans were such a novelty to Spanish explorers and clerics in the 1500s that some considered the legumes a delicacy for the nobility.

Mixed with roasted corn kernels and bell peppers, then marinated in spices, chile, and lime juice, black beans become a colorful and filling salad.

Serves 4 to 6

6 ears corn, husked, or 3 cups frozen corn, thawed
2 cups cooked black beans (*page 166*), drained,
    or canned black beans, drained and rinsed
½ cup diced red bell pepper
½ cup diced yellow bell pepper
1 teaspoon minced garlic
¼ cup chopped fresh cilantro
1 tablespoon seeded and minced jalapeño chile
1 teaspoon ground cumin
1 teaspoon ground coriander
3 tablespoons fresh lime juice
3 tablespoons corn or canola oil
Salt to taste

Preheat the oven to 350°F. If using fresh corn, place the ears directly on the oven rack. If using frozen corn, spread the thawed kernels on a rimmed baking sheet and pat dry with paper towels. Roast for 8 to 10 minutes, or until beginning to color. Remove from the oven and let cool to the touch. Cut the kernels from the corncobs if using fresh corn. Transfer corn to a large bowl. Add the beans, bell peppers, garlic, cilantro, jalapeño, cumin, and coriander and toss to coat. Add the lime juice and oil and toss again. Season with salt. Serve at room temperature, or cover and refrigerate for at least 2 hours, or up to 2 days.

QUINOA SALAD

Quinoa is a high-altitude plant grown in the Andes both for its leaves and its protein-rich seeds. Second only to maize and potatoes in the Inka diet, both parts of the plant were added to soups and stews. Quinoa seeds, which are most commonly white or yellow, also were toasted, ground, and made into breads.

Here, the cooked seeds are tossed with fresh tomatoes, cucumbers, cilantro, and scallions and dressed with a lemon-honey vinaigrette.

SERVES 4 TO 6

Lemon Vinaigrette
½ cup fresh lemon juice
¼ cup honey
1½ cups canola oil
Salt and freshly ground pepper to taste

Salad
2 cups white or yellow quinoa, rinsed
5 cups water
½ yellow onion
1 stalk celery, cut into 3-inch pieces
1 carrot, peeled and cut into 3-inch pieces
1 bay leaf
2 plum (Roma) tomatoes, finely diced (1 cup)
2 cucumbers, seeded and finely diced (2 cups)
¼ cup minced fresh cilantro
4 to 5 scallions, including some green parts, chopped

For the vinaigrette: In a small bowl, combine the lemon juice and honey. Gradually whisk in the oil until incorporated. Season with salt and pepper.

For the salad: In a large saucepan, combine the quinoa, water, onion, celery, carrot, and bay leaf. Bring to a boil and cook over medium heat for 15 minutes, or until the quinoa grains are translucent and tender. Remove from the heat and drain in a fine-meshed sieve. Remove and discard the vegetables and bay leaf and let the quinoa cool.

In a large bowl, combine the cooked quinoa, tomatoes, cucumbers, cilantro, and scallions. Toss to mix. Add the vinaigrette to the salad and toss to coat. Serve at room temperature or chilled.

Hominy Salad
with Saffron Vinaigrette

According to John Smith, the founder of the first permanent settlement in Virginia, the Algonquian-speaking tribes used the word *ustatahamen* to describe fresh or dried corn kernels that had been boiled in water with wood ashes or slaked lime to remove their hulls. While scholars still debate the accuracy of Smith's transcription, corn that has undergone similar treatment is today called hominy, or, in Mesoamerica, pozole.

At the Mitsitam Cafe, hominy is often served in this bright yellow salad with pearl onions and sun-dried tomatoes.

Serves 4 to 6

Saffron Vinaigrette
  2 tablespoons cider vinegar
  1 tablespoon Dijon mustard
  1 small shallot, minced
  1 teaspoon powdered saffron or saffron threads mixed with ¼ cup hot water
  ½ cup corn or canola oil
  Salt and freshly ground pepper to taste

Salad
  1 pound dried hominy (hulled pozole) (*see Ingredients and Sources, page 171*)
  1 teaspoon powdered saffron or saffron threads
  ½ cup pearl onions
  1½ tablespoons corn or canola oil
  ¼ cup finely chopped arugula
  ¼ cup oil-packed sun-dried tomatoes, drained and quartered
  ½ teaspoon minced garlic

For the vinaigrette: In a small bowl combine the vinegar, mustard, shallots, and saffron mixture. Gradually whisk in the oil until incorporated.

For the salad: Put the hominy in a large pot and add water to cover. Bring to a boil, stir in the teaspoon of saffron, and reduce the heat to medium. Cook at a brisk simmer until the hominy opens and is tender, 1 to 1¼ hours, adding more water as needed to keep the hominy covered. Remove from the heat and let cool in its liquid. Meanwhile, preheat the oven to 350°F. Peel the pearl onions and put them in a small bowl. Add the oil and toss to coat. Spread the onions in a small baking pan and roast in the oven until lightly browned, 10 to 15 minutes. Remove from the oven and set aside.

Drain the hominy. In a large bowl, combine the hominy, roasted onions, arugula, tomatoes, and garlic. Toss to mix. Add the vinaigrette and toss to coat.

SMOKED TROUT AND WATERCRESS SALAD

Most Plains communities kept their culinary focus on venison and, more importantly, buffalo. But trout was abundant in the streams and small rivers that fed into the Missouri and Mississippi, and it was occasionally caught and roasted over a fire. The riverbanks also yielded a variety of edible wild greens, including miner's lettuce and watercress.

Stockbridge-Munsee silver tie tack depicting a muskellunge fish, 1964. Bowler, Stockbridge-Munsee Reservation, Wisconsin. Indian Arts and Crafts Board Collection, Department of the Interior, at the National Museum of the American Indian, Smithsonian Institution. 25/7991

SERVES 4 TO 6

Raspberry Vinaigrette
¼ cup raspberry vinegar
¾ cup canola oil
2 tablespoons walnut oil

Salad
2 cups watercress sprigs
1 cup frisée lettuce leaves
½ Granny Smith apple, peeled, cored, and cut into 2-inch matchsticks
1 beet, peeled and cut into 2-inch matchsticks (optional)
¼ cup dried currants
2 radishes, thinly sliced
¼ cup pumpkin seeds, toasted and cooled (*page 167*)
Salt and freshly ground pepper to taste
10 to 12 ounces smoked trout, broken into 1-inch pieces
¼ cup chopped walnuts, toasted and cooled (*page 167*)

For the vinaigrette: Put the vinegar in a small bowl and gradually whisk in the canola oil. Whisk in the walnut oil and set aside.

For the salad: In a medium bowl, combine the watercress, frisée, apple, beet (if using), currants, radishes, and pumpkin seeds. Toss to mix. Add the vinaigrette and toss to coat. Season with salt and pepper. Top each serving with an equal amount of the trout and walnuts.

Smoked Duck Salad

Smoked Duck Salad

Along the North Pacific Coast, migrating wild ducks each spring provided people with the first fresh meat in the annual food cycle. Native communities had varying techniques for capturing the ducks. The S'Klallam people of the Olympic Peninsula in present-day Washington State erected 40-foot-high poles strung with fine net into which flocks of ducks would fly in the dim light of dawn or sunset. Other Coast Salish hunters tied nets between trees, and the Makah submerged netting covered with salmon eggs in lakes and streams where the ducks typically fed.

In this salad, smoked duck is balanced with the earthy taste of beets and the sweetness of apple and dried cherries.

Serves 4 to 6

Apple Cider Vinaigrette
    6 tablespoons apple cider vinegar
    ¼ cup honey
    ¾ cup canola oil
    Salt and freshly ground pepper to taste

Salad
    2 cups baby spinach leaves
    1 cup frisée lettuce leaves
    2 red or golden beets, peeled and cut into 2-inch matchsticks
    1 Granny Smith apple, peeled, cored, and cut into 2-inch matchsticks
    ¼ cup dried cherries
    10 to 12 ounces smoked duck breast (*see Ingredients and Sources, page 171*), cut into thin slices
    ¼ cup pine nuts, toasted and cooled (*page 167*)

For the vinaigrette: In a small bowl, combine all the ingredients and whisk to blend. Cover and refrigerate for at least 1 hour, or up to 10 days.

For the salad: In a large bowl, combine the spinach, frisée, beets, apple, and dried cherries. Toss to mix. Add ½ cup vinaigrette and toss to coat. Top each serving with the smoked duck and pine nuts.

Main Courses

Earnest L. Spybuck (Absentee Shawnee, 1883–1949),
Cornbread Dance, *1908–1910. Shawnee, Oklahoma.*
Watercolor on paperboard, 63.3 x 50.5 cm. 2/6927. Held in the
spring and fall, the Bread Dance is the central ceremonial event
for Shawnees, a celebration of the earth's gifts. In the early 1900s,
the men prepared for the feast with three days of hunting. Two
days of dancing and feasting followed. In the foreground of this
painting, the women unpack the deer, turkey, and other game
that the men have caught.

CORN AND TOMATO STEW

Tomatoes originated in South America, with seven species growing wild from Chile to Ecuador. Their seeds, carried northward probably by birds, may have arrived in Mexico as early as 800 BC. Aztec farmers found the fruit better suited to lowland growing conditions than the more familiar green husk tomato, or tomatillo, a native of Mesoamerica. Red tomatoes, however, were slow to gain acceptance in North America and Europe, where many considered them poisonous. Although British horticulturalists had been experimenting with tomato plants since the 1700s, the fruit was still a curiosity in northern Europe and North America at the turn of the 20th century.

Combined with corn kernels and flavored with epazote, these red tomatoes make a hearty stew.

SERVES 4 TO 6

Sofrito
1 cup chopped red bell pepper
1 cup chopped green bell pepper
1 yellow onion, chopped
4 plum (Roma) tomatoes, chopped
2 garlic cloves, minced

Stew
¼ cup corn or canola oil
½ cup diced carrot
1 cup diced yellow onion
½ cup diced celery
¼ cup minced garlic (8 to 10 cloves)
3 cups fresh corn kernels (about 6 ears)
    or 3 cups frozen, thawed corn kernels
1 russet potato, peeled and diced
8 cups homemade vegetable stock (*page 165*)
    or canned low-sodium vegetable stock
2 cups canned diced tomatoes with juice
Salt and freshly ground pepper to taste
¼ cup minced fresh epazote (*see Ingredients and Sources, page 171*)
    or cilantro

For the sofrito: Combine all the sofrito ingredients in a blender or food processor and puree until smooth.

For the stew: In a large soup pot, heat the oil over medium heat and sauté the carrot, onion, celery, and garlic until the onion is translucent, about 3 minutes. Add the sofrito, corn kernels, and potato to the sautéed vegetable mixture and cook, stirring occasionally, for 20 to 30 minutes. Add the vegetable stock and the canned tomatoes and their juice and simmer for 20 to 30 minutes.

Puree one-fourth of the soup in a blender until smooth. Return to the pot and reheat briefly. Season with salt and pepper. Divide the soup among 4 to 6 deep bowls. Garnish with the epazote or cilantro and serve.

BUFFALO CHILI

SERVES 6 TO 8

When an interviewer asked Pretty Shield, a Crow medicine woman who told wonderful stories about the days when her tribe followed the buffalo, why she had no stories about the time after the tribe moved to the reservation, she said there was nothing to tell. For the Crow, and for most Plains tribes, buffalo still represent freedom. By the 1890s, non-Native hunters had reduced North America's buffalo population to only 1,500 animals, but in succeeding decades, herds have gradually expanded on their former ranges. Today, buffalo (more accurately known as the North American bison) is raised commercially and is prized for its low-fat meat.

This deeply flavored chili is made with ground buffalo and thickened with masa harina.

Sumner W. Matteson Jr. (1867–1920). A herd of buffalo, ca. 1890. Probably Fort Belknap Reservation, Montana. P32392

2 tablespoons canola oil
1 pound ground buffalo meat (*see Ingredients and Sources, page 171*)
1 yellow onion, chopped
1 green bell pepper, chopped
2 chipotle chiles en adobo, minced (*see Ingredients and Sources, page 171*)
1 to 2 tablespoons ground cumin
2 tablespoons ground coriander
¼ cup chili powder
1 tablespoon minced garlic
1 28-ounce can diced tomatoes
1 cup tomato puree
2 cups cooked pinto beans (*page 167*), drained,
    or canned pinto beans, drained and rinsed
1 cup water
1 cup beef stock, plus more if necessary
2 tablespoons tomato paste
½ cup masa harina (*see Ingredients and Sources, page 171*)
Salt and freshly ground pepper to taste

In a Dutch oven or heavy soup pot, heat the oil and cook the ground buffalo over medium heat, breaking it up with a spoon, until well browned and crumbled. Add the onion, bell pepper, chiles, cumin, coriander, chili powder, and garlic. Sauté until the onion is translucent, about 3 minutes.

Stir in the tomatoes and tomato puree; bring to a simmer and cook for 15 minutes. Add the pinto beans, water, and beef stock. Bring to a boil over high heat, then reduce the heat to a simmer and cook for 30 minutes. Stir in the tomato paste and simmer 30 minutes more. Gradually stir in the masa harina to thicken lightly. Add more water or stock if the chili becomes too thick. Season with salt and pepper. Simmer for 15 minutes.

LOBSTER ROLLS

Native cooks along the North Atlantic Coast, especially among the Penobscots and Narragansetts, prepared a clambake by digging a pit in the sand, lining it with stones, and building a wood fire over the stones. When the fire had burned down, the cooks would layer wet seaweed over the hot stones and then fill the pit with layers of clams, potatoes, lobsters, and corn, each layer separated by more seaweed. The food would then steam in the clean salt water and its own juices. Among the Wampanoag and in other Native communities in the Northeast today, very similar clambakes still are held to mark festivals and other special occasions.

In this classic sandwich, watercress and radishes are added to a mixture of lobster meat and creamy dressing.

Note: *Lobster rolls are made with New England–style hot dog buns that are split along the top rather than on the side. If you can't find them, use any soft sandwich rolls.*

MAKES 4 ROLLS

½ cup mayonnaise
1 tablespoon sour cream
1 tablespoon Dijon mustard
½ teaspoon curry powder
1 teaspoon minced fresh dill
2 scallions, including some green parts, finely chopped
¼ cup finely diced tomato
¼ cup finely diced celery
1 pound cooked lobster meat, diced
¼ cup chopped radishes
Cayenne pepper to taste
4 New England–style hot dog rolls or other sandwich rolls
½ bunch watercress, stemmed

In a medium bowl, combine the mayonnaise, sour cream, mustard, curry powder, dill, scallions, tomato, and celery. Stir to blend. Fold in the lobster, radishes, and cayenne.

Cut each roll about three-fourths of the way through the center and open like a book. Fill each roll with one-fourth of the watercress, then one-fourth of the lobster mixture.

SMOKED TROUT AND DANDELION GREEN SANDWICHES

As most gardeners know, dandelions grow nearly anywhere. They are harvested in spring, when the new leaves are tender. Many Native communities have a long tradition of using dandelion greens, either cooked in soups or eaten raw, mixed with other wild greens. Their slightly bitter flavor contrasts beautifully with smoked trout in these sandwiches, along with crunchy apple and celery root.

Mary Benson (Pomo 1878–1930). Cooking basket, ca. 1905. Ukiah, California. Twined sedge and redbud, 42 cm. x 24.5 cm. 24/2107

MAKES 4 SANDWICHES

Dressing
¼ cup mayonnaise
¼ cup sour cream
Salt and freshly ground pepper to taste

Sandwiches
8 ounces smoked trout, broken into 1-inch pieces
½ Granny Smith apple, peeled, cored,
    and cut into 2-inch matchsticks
¼ cup celery root (celeriac), peeled and
    cut into 2-inch matchsticks
    (*see Ingredients and Sources, page 171*)
2 scallions, including some green parts, chopped
1 tablespoon fresh lemon juice
Salt and freshly ground pepper to taste
1½ small bunches (3 to 4 ounces) dandelion greens
    (*see Ingredients and Sources, page 171*)
8 slices walnut-raisin or sourdough bread

For the dressing: Combine all the ingredients in a small bowl and stir to blend.

For the sandwiches: In a medium bowl, combine the trout, apple, celery root, scallions, and lemon juice. Gently toss to blend. Add the dressing and toss gently to coat. Season with salt and pepper.

Divide the dandelion greens among 4 slices of the bread and top each with one-fourth of the trout mixture. Top with the remaining slices of bread. Cut each sandwich in half on the diagonal and serve.

Juniper-Cured Salmon Sandwich

Juniper-Cured Salmon Sandwiches

Along the North Pacific Coast, from Oregon to southeastern Alaska, Native communities relied on the ocean and rivers for the bulk of their food supply. Salmon were especially abundant, with five to seven "runs" up coastal rivers each year. During the salmon season, entire communities worked together to catch, clean, smoke, dry, and store the fish as quickly as possible for use throughout the year.

Instead of being smoked, the salmon here is "cooked" using a curing process that imbues it with the foresty aroma of juniper berries. The sandwiches are served with watercress and a spicy horseradish dressing.

Note: *You will need to cure the salmon for 24 hours before making these sandwiches.*

3 tablespoons dried juniper berries
　　(*see Ingredients and Sources, page 171*)
2 cups kosher salt
2 cups sugar
1 8-ounce salmon fillet, pin bones removed
2 tablespoons prepared horseradish
¼ cup sour cream
8 slices whole-grain bread
½ cup very thinly sliced cucumber
1 cup watercress sprigs
Freshly ground black pepper to taste

In a spice grinder or mortar, grind the juniper berries to a powder. Put the ground juniper in a medium bowl and add the salt and sugar. Stir to blend.

Cut a 2-foot length of cheesecloth and double it over to a 1-foot length. Place half of the salt mixture in the center of the cloth and place the salmon on top, pressing it into the salt mixture so that the salt mixture covers the bottom of the fish. Place the remaining salt mixture on top of the fish. Wrap the cheesecloth tightly around the fish.

Place the fish in a roasting pan and set a smaller roasting pan or baking dish on top, open side up. Weight the smaller pan with about 2½ pounds of canned goods or a small, heavy skillet. Refrigerate for 24 hours.

Remove the fish from the cloth and rinse off the salt mixture. The fish should now be opaque, and the skin can be easily sliced off with a sharp knife. Cut the salmon into very thin diagonal slices.

In a small bowl, combine the horseradish and sour cream. Stir to blend. Spread the horseradish cream on one side of each bread slice. Layer the cucumber over 4 of the bread slices and top with the sliced salmon. Sprinkle the salmon on each sandwich very generously with pepper; top with the watercress, then with the remaining bread slices.

Heat a large grill pan over medium heat and spray with cooking spray. Toast the sandwiches, in batches, for 3 to 5 minutes on each side. Serve hot.

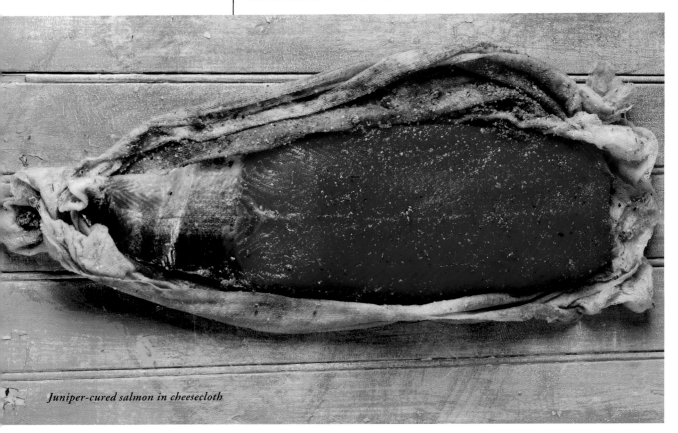

Juniper-cured salmon in cheesecloth

ASH-ROASTED CHICKEN BREAST SANDWICHES

Roasting or steaming packets of food directly in the embers is a technique common to many indigenous cooking traditions. Native Hawaiians wrap fish in ti or banana leaves and steam them over embers covered with seaweed. In the Yucatán region of Mexico, marinated pork is wrapped in banana leaves or damp corn husks and, like the chicken in this recipe, buried in hot ashes to cook in its flavorful juices.

Caramelized onions and a sauce of strawberries and pumpkin add intense flavors to these aromatic open-faced sandwiches.

Note: *You will need 3 cups mesquite or hickory wood chips for this recipe. Although the ashes of a charcoal fire are necessary to cook this dish authentically, a gas grill may also be used.*

MAKES 4 OPEN-FACED SANDWICHES

Marinade
¼ cup canola oil
2 teaspoons minced fresh thyme
1 teaspoon minced fresh rosemary

Sandwiches
4 boneless, skinless chicken breast halves
    (about 6 ounces each)
1 banana leaf, or 8 fresh or dried corn husks
    (see *Ingredients and Sources, page 171*)
3 tablespoons canola oil
2 yellow onions, thinly sliced
Salt and freshly ground pepper to taste
1 cup fresh strawberries
¼ cup pumpkin puree
4 slices jalapeño cheese bread or sourdough rolls
6 or 8 arugula leaves

For the marinade: In a large bowl, combine all the ingredients.

For the sandwiches: Add the chicken to the marinade, turn to coat, and let stand at room temperature for 1 hour. Prepare a medium fire in a charcoal grill, or preheat a gas grill to medium. Soak the wood chips in water to cover for 30 minutes. Cut the banana leaf into 4 pieces, with each piece measuring about 10 inches wide and 8 inches long. If using dried corn husks, soak them in hot water for 30 minutes; drain, and pat dry.

Meanwhile, in a medium skillet, heat 2 tablespoons of the oil over medium heat and cook the onions, stirring occasionally, until caramelized, about 25 minutes. Remove from the heat and set aside.

Remove the chicken from the marinade and season with salt and pepper. Wrap each chicken breast half in a banana leaf piece or 2 overlapping corn husks, folding it like a package.

Drain the wood chips. If using a charcoal grill, sprinkle them over the coals (this will produce a lot of smoke); if using a gas grill, poke a few holes in the bottom of a disposable aluminum pan, add the drained chips to the pan, and place the pan on top of the lava rocks. Place the chicken packets in the coals and cover with the hot ashes of a charcoal fire, or place them among the smoking wood chips in the heated pan in the gas grill. Cover the grill. Cook for 25 to 30 minutes, or until an instant-read thermometer inserted in a packet registers 155°F. Remove from the grill and let cool slightly.

Meanwhile, in a medium sauté pan, sauté the strawberries in the remaining 1 tablespoon oil over medium heat for 6 to 8 minutes, or until soft. Transfer to a blender, add the pumpkin puree, and blend until smooth, thinning with a little warm water if necessary. Season with salt and pepper to taste.

To serve, unwrap the chicken. Spread one side of each bread slice or roll with the strawberry-pumpkin spread. Top with arugula, then the chicken, then the caramelized onion. Serve at once.

Probably Sioux beaded deer hide dress, ca. 1865. South Dakota. 5/958

Carne Asada Sandwiches
with Chimichurri Sauce

With its abundant prairies of pampas grasses, Argentina is home to South America's largest cattle industry. Although the original gauchos (cowboys) were descendants of the Spanish conquistadors, the indigenous Mapuche people, who live along the Chile-Argentine frontier, prepare lamb *asado* (barbecue) much as the gauchos did. They skewer large cuts of meat on thin metal poles and use a crosspiece to keep each piece of meat flat. The skewers are driven into the ground and tilted at an angle toward a wood fire. In this recipe, as in most of South America today, a grill has replaced the traditional skewers.

The beef in this recipe is marinated in a mixture of citrus juice and herbs before being grilled and served with *chimichurri*, the classic Argentine green sauce of parsley and cilantro.

Makes 4 sandwiches

Chimichurri Sauce
    1 cup packed fresh flat-leaf parsley leaves
    ¼ cup packed fresh cilantro leaves
    ½ cup olive oil
    2 garlic cloves
    ¾ teaspoon red pepper flakes
    ½ teaspoon Dijon mustard
    ½ teaspoon ground cumin
    ½ teaspoon salt
    ⅓ cup white wine vinegar
    1 or 2 tablespoons water (optional)

Marinade
    2 cups corn or canola oil
    1 cup chopped fresh oregano
    1 cup fresh orange juice
    1 cup fresh lime juice
    1 cup cider vinegar
    1 unpeeled orange, scrubbed and cut into slices

Sandwiches
    1½ pounds beef skirt steak, trimmed
    Salt and freshly ground pepper to taste
    4 pieces pita or lavash bread
    16 large arugula leaves
    1 tomato, cut into slices

For the chimichurri sauce: In a blender, combine the parsley, cilantro, and olive oil and puree until smooth. Transfer the puree to a large glass measuring cup. Rinse and dry the blender. Add the garlic, red pepper flakes, mustard, cumin, salt, and vinegar and puree until smooth. With the machine running, gradually drizzle in the herb oil until the mixture is emulsified. Add a tablespoon or two of water if the mixture is too thick. Use immediately, or cover and refrigerate for up to 1 week.

For the marinade: In a large bowl, combine all the ingredients.

For the sandwiches: Add the meat to the marinade and turn to coat. Cover and refrigerate for 24 hours, turning several times. Remove the meat from the refrigerator and the bowl, reserving the marinade. Season with salt and pepper. Prepare a hot fire in a charcoal grill or preheat a gas grill to high.

Place the steak on the grill and top with the orange slices from the marinade. Spoon some of the reserved marinade on top. Grill for 3 to 4 minutes, then remove the orange slices and turn the steak over. Top with the orange slices, spoon some of the reserved marinade over, and cook for 3 to 4 minutes on the second side for medium-rare. Transfer the steak to a carving board, tent with aluminum foil, and let rest for 8 to 10 minutes.

Meanwhile, grill the bread until heated and lightly crisped, about 1½ minutes on each side. Transfer to a plate and keep warm.

Cut the steak against the grain into thin slices. Spread 2 tablespoons of the chimichurri sauce on the top of each piece of flat bread and top with 4 arugula leaves and 2 or 3 tomato slices, then one-fourth of the sliced steak. Top with 1 to 2 tablespoons of the sauce. Roll up the bread. Serve at once.

PULLED BUFFALO SANDWICHES
WITH CHAYOTE SLAW

Chayote, which looks like a very large pear and has a taste similar to that of summer squash, is native to Mesoamerica and the Caribbean. A thick and aggressive vine, it has been cultivated by indigenous people for centuries.

In this recipe, its mild flavor is a foil to buffalo brisket, cooked until falling-apart tender and served with a vinegary barbecue sauce.

MAKES 6 SANDWICHES

Buffalo Filling

¼ cup corn or canola oil

3½ pounds buffalo brisket, cut into 3-inch cubes

6 to 8 cups water

2 cups distilled white vinegar

½ cup chopped yellow onion

¼ cup minced garlic (8 to 10 cloves)

¼ cup sugar

1 tablespoon salt

1 tablespoon freshly ground pepper

¼ cup red pepper flakes

¼ cup chili powder

¼ cup dry mustard

Barbecue Sauce

1½ cups distilled white vinegar

¾ cup packed brown sugar

2 tablespoons red pepper flakes

½ yellow onion, chopped

1 cinnamon stick

2 tablespoons chili powder

4 cloves

6 whole-wheat sandwich rolls, split and toasted

Chayote Slaw for serving (recipe follows)

Preheat the oven to 325°F. In a large Dutch oven or heavy casserole, heat the oil over medium-high heat just until smoking and sauté the buffalo in batches until browned on all sides, about 6 minutes per batch. Using a slotted spoon, transfer each batch to a bowl and set aside. When all the meat is browned, return it to the pan. Add the water, vinegar, onion, garlic, sugar,

Pulled Buffalo Sandwich with Chayote Slaw

salt, and spices. Stir to blend. The liquid should just barely cover the meat. Cover and bake until the meat is falling-apart tender, 4 to 6 hours.

Meanwhile, make the barbecue sauce: In a large nonreactive pot, combine all the ingredients. Bring to a boil over medium heat, then reduce the heat to a brisk simmer and cook for 10 minutes. Remove from the heat and let cool.

Remove the meat from the oven. Using a slotted spoon, transfer the meat to a plate and let cool slightly, discarding the liquid. Pull the meat into bite-sized chunks and transfer to a medium bowl. Add the barbecue sauce and stir to mix.

Serve on toasted, split, whole-wheat buns, topped with the chayote slaw.

Chayote Slaw

Makes 6 servings

> 1 chayote, peeled, seeded, and cut into 2-inch matchsticks
> (*see Ingredients and Sources, page 171*)
> ¼ cup carrots cut into 2-inch matchsticks
> ¼ cup fresh cilantro leaves
> 3 tablespoons fresh lime juice
> Salt and freshly ground pepper to taste

In a medium bowl, combine the chayote, carrot, and cilantro. Add the lime juice and toss to coat. Season with salt and pepper and toss again.

Ingredients for Pork Pibil Tacos and Beef Adobo Tacos

Tacos

As recorded in the 1500s by the Spanish friar Bernardino de
Sahagún, Aztec cuisine included an array of maize tortillas
that extended far beyond the simple corn and flour varieties
known to most North Americans today. Thin, thick, large,
small, soft, rough, wide, narrow, and layered are just a
few of the adjectives the priest used to described the flat,
unleavened corn breads eaten by the nobility. Commoners
had less variety, but they probably ate tortillas more than
any other food. In Aztec markets, food sellers offered
tortillas (folded or not) with beans, chiles, corn, meats,
vegetables, and a wide variety of sauces. These tortilla-
based "street foods" are the ancestors of today's take-out
burritos and tacos.

CHICKEN MOLE VERDE TACOS

Mole verde is made of fresh herbs and tomatillos—small, green, tomatolike fruits that grow inside papery husks. Tomatillos are native to the Mesoamerican highlands and were an established part of the Aztec diet by the time the Spanish arrived in the 1500s. Nearly every region of Mexico has its own version of mole verde, or green mole, with each incorporating local produce. This sauce is excellent with both pork and chicken, as in these tacos.

Note: *The mole verde used in this recipe may be made up to 3 days ahead of time.*

MAKES 8 TACOS

Tacos

2 pounds boneless, skinless chicken thighs
1 cup sliced yellow onion
1 cup chopped green bell pepper
2 cups fresh orange juice
2 cups water
1 cup chopped fresh cilantro
½ cup fresh lemon juice
¼ cup minced garlic (8 to 10 cloves)
Salt to taste
2 cups Mole Verde (*page 134*)
8 corn tortilla shells or 8 soft flour tortillas

Toppings

½ cup grated cotija cheese, crumbled queso fresco, or feta cheese
½ cup sour cream
½ cup Guacamole (*page 10*)
½ cup Salsa of choice (*pages 128–33*)

Preheat the oven to 350°F. In a Dutch oven or heavy casserole, combine the chicken, onion, bell pepper, orange juice, water, cilantro, lemon juice, garlic, and salt. Cover and bake for 1½ to 2 hours, or until the chicken is tender. Remove from the oven.

Using a slotted spoon, transfer the meat to a plate and let cool slightly, discarding the liquid. Shred the chicken into bite-sized pieces. Add the mole verde. Taste and adjust the seasoning.

If using flour tortillas, heat a dry 12-inch sauté pan over medium-high heat for several seconds. Heat each tortilla separately, turning once, for about 30 seconds per side. Keep warm in a low oven on a baking sheet, layering the tortillas with clean dish towels to keep them from sticking together.

To serve, divide the chicken among the tortillas, top with cheese, sour cream, guacamole, and salsa choice. If using flour tortillas, fold one side over about 2 inches of the filling and roll. Alternatively, if the tortillas are small, fold in half.

PORK PIBIL TACOS

The *pib*, or pit, is the basis of an ancient roasting technique that also has cultural meaning for Maya people: offerings (such as meat, special tamales, or new ears of corn) to agricultural spirits must be cooked in the heart of the earth. The Yucatecan method is to dig a deep pit, line it with hardwood kindling, cover the wood with an even layer of shatterproof stones, and light the wood fire. When the stones are hot, the cooks place pans of food on them, covering everything with oak branches and a sheet of corrugated metal. Dirt is shoveled on top, and the food cooks undisturbed for more than an hour.

Here, pork shoulder is braised with oranges, limes, garlic, and chiles in a heavy covered casserole, an indoor version of the pit.

MAKES 8 TACOS

Tacos
- ¼ cup corn or canola oil
- 3 pounds boneless pork shoulder (pork butt), cut into 4-inch cubes
- 1 cup coarsely chopped onion
- ¼ cup minced garlic (8 to 10 cloves)
- ¼ cup seeded and coarsely chopped jalapeño chiles
- 2 unpeeled oranges, cut into wedges
- 2 unpeeled limes, cut into wedges
- 1 teaspoon ground cumin
- 4 cups water
- Salt and freshly ground pepper to taste
- 1 cup chopped fresh cilantro
- 8 corn tortilla shells or 8 soft flour tortillas

Toppings
- ½ cup grated cotija cheese, crumbled queso fresco, or feta cheese
- ½ cup sour cream
- ½ cup Guacamole (*page 10*)
- ½ cup Salsa of choice (*pages 128–33*)

Preheat the oven to 300°F. In a Dutch oven or heavy casserole, heat the oil over medium-high heat until smoking and brown the pork, in batches, on all sides, about 6 minutes per batch. Using a slotted spoon, transfer each batch to a bowl; when all the meat is browned, return it to the pan. Add the onion, garlic, chiles, oranges, limes, cumin, water, salt, pepper, and half of the cilantro. Cover and bake for about 4 hours, or until very tender. Remove from the oven.

Using a slotted spoon, transfer the meat and vegetables to a plate, reserving the liquid, and let the meat cool to the touch. Discard the orange and lime wedges.

Pull the meat apart into bite-sized chunks. Meanwhile, place the pan on the stove and cook the pan liquid over medium heat until reduced by half.

Return the meat and vegetables to the reduced liquid. Stir in the remaining cilantro. Taste and adjust the seasoning. Reheat the mixture over medium-low heat.

If using flour tortillas, heat a dry 12-inch sauté pan over medium-high heat for several seconds. Heat each tortilla separately, turning once, for about 30 seconds per side. Keep warm in a low oven on a baking sheet, layering the tortillas with clean dish towels to keep them from sticking together.

To serve, divide the pork among the tortillas, top with cheese, sour cream, guacamole, and salsa choice, and (if using flour tortillas) fold one side over about 2 inches of the filling and roll. Alternatively, if the tortillas are small, fold them in half.

Maya ceramic tripod bowl, AD 300–650.
Yucatán, Mexico. 33.8 x 9.4 cm. 24/6499

PULLED PORK TACOS

MAKES 8 TACOS

A key ingredient in this taco filling is chipotle chiles en adobo. With a name that derives from the Nahuatl word for "smoked chile," chipotles are smoked jalapeños. Their deep, hot taste flavors pork shoulder braised with bell peppers, orange juice, and cilantro.

Tacos

- ¼ cup corn or canola oil
- 3 pounds boneless pork shoulder (pork butt), cut into 3-inch cubes
- 1 cup sliced green bell pepper
- 1 cup sliced red bell pepper
- 1 cup sliced onion
- 4 cups fresh orange juice
- 4 to 5 chipotle chiles en adobo, chopped, adobo sauce reserved
- 1 cup minced fresh cilantro
- 2 teaspoons ground cumin
- 2 teaspoons ground coriander
- 1 teaspoon red pepper flakes
- 2 cups water
- Salt and freshly ground pepper to taste
- 8 corn tortilla shells or 8 soft flour tortillas

Toppings

- ½ cup grated cotija cheese, crumbled queso fresco, or feta cheese
- ½ cup sour cream
- ½ cup Guacamole (*page 10*)
- ½ cup Salsa of choice (*pages 128–33*)

Preheat the oven to 300°F. In a Dutch oven or heavy casserole, heat the oil over medium-high heat until smoking and brown the pork, in batches, on all sides, about 6 minutes per batch. Using a slotted spoon, transfer each batch to a bowl. When all the meat is browned, return it to the pan. Add the green and red bell peppers, onion, 2 cups of the orange juice, 2 or 3 of the chiles, half of the cilantro, and all of the cumin, coriander, red pepper flakes, water, salt, and pepper.

Cover and bake until tender, about 6 hours. Using a slotted spoon, transfer the meat and vegetables to a plate, reserving liquid. Let the meat cool to the touch, then pull it apart into bite-sized chunks. Meanwhile, place the pan over medium-high heat and cook to reduce the pan liquid by half. Return the meat and vegetables to the reduced liquid. Add the remaining 2 cups orange juice, the reserved adobo sauce, and the remaining chiles and cilantro. Taste and adjust the seasoning. Reheat the mixture over medium-low heat.

Meanwhile, if using flour tortillas, heat a dry 12-inch sauté pan over medium-high heat for several seconds. Heat each tortilla separately, turning once, for about 30 seconds per side. Keep warm in a low oven on a baking sheet, layering the tortillas with clean dish towels to keep them from sticking together.

To serve, divide the pork among the tortillas, top with cheese, sour cream, guacamole, and salsa choice. If using flour tortillas, fold one side over about 2 inches of the filling and roll. Alternatively, if the tortillas are small, fold in half.

BEEF ADOBO TACOS

According to Aztec tribute lists that date to the 1550s, the Spanish governor of Coyoacán in the Valley of Mexico received every week a shipment that included 700 tomatoes and 700 chiles. This slow-cooked beef brisket features not only the classic Aztec combination of tomatoes and chiles but also a variation of Mesoamerican adobo sauce made of ground chiles, spices, herbs, and lime juice.

Makes 8 tacos

Tacos
¼ cup corn or canola oil
3 pounds beef brisket, cut into 4-inch cubes
1 poblano chile, seeded, deribbed, and cut into l-inch dice
    (*see Ingredients and Sources, page 171*)
½ cup chopped yellow onion
1 cup canned diced tomatoes with juice
1 tablespoon minced garlic
¼ cup pine nuts
¼ cup chopped pecans
¼ cup chopped raw almonds
1 tablespoon fresh lime juice
1 teaspoon ground cinnamon
1 teaspoon ground aniseed
1 teaspoon ground cumin
Salt and freshly ground pepper to taste
4 cups water
8 corn tortilla shells or 8 soft flour tortillas

Toppings
½ cup grated cotija cheese, crumbled queso fresco, or feta cheese
½ cup sour cream
½ cup Guacamole (*page 10*)
½ cup Salsa of choice (*pages 128–33*)

Preheat the oven to 300°F. In a Dutch oven or heavy casserole, heat oil over medium-high heat just until smoking and brown the meat, in batches, on all sides, about 6 minutes per batch. Using a slotted spoon, transfer each batch to a bowl. When all the meat is browned, return it to the pan and add all the remaining ingredients except the tortillas and toppings. Cover and bake until the meat is fork-tender, 8 to 10 hours.

Remove from the oven. Using a slotted spoon, transfer the meat and vegetables to a platter, reserving liquid. Let the meat cool to the touch, then shred it into bite-sized pieces.

Return the meat to the pan and add 1 to 1½ cups of the cooking liquid. Reheat over medium-low heat.

If using flour tortillas, heat a dry 12-inch sauté pan over medium-high heat for several seconds. Heat each tortilla separately, turning once, for about 30 seconds per side. Keep warm in a low oven on a baking sheet, layering the tortillas with clean dish towels to keep them from sticking together.

To serve, divide the beef among the tortillas and top with the cheese, sour cream, guacamole, and salsa choice. If using flour tortillas, fold one side over about 2 inches of the filling and roll. Alternatively, if the tortillas are small, fold in half.

Fry Bread Tacos

FRY BREAD TACOS

Fry bread tacos—also known as Indian tacos or Navajo tacos—are essential Native festival food throughout the United States. At fairs, powwows, and community events, a piece of hot fry bread is topped with a combination of meat, cheese, lettuce, tomato, and chiles, and is eaten as soon as it is made. Considered to have originated with the Diné (Navajo), fry bread tacos are probably one of the best known of all Native dishes, but every community has its own version. Here, buffalo chili provides the meat base.

MAKES 4 TACOS

Tacos
    4 pieces freshly made plain Fry Bread (*page 141*)
    1½ cups Buffalo Chili (*page 63*)

Toppings
    ¼ cup shredded lettuce
    ¼ cup diced tomato
    ¼ cup shredded Cheddar cheese
    3 or 4 jalapeño chile slices
    2 tablespoons finely diced red onion (optional)

Place each piece of fry bread on a plate and top with one-fourth of all the remaining ingredients in the order listed. Serve at once.

BAKED BLACK BEAN AND SPINACH BURRITOS

Black beans were one of at least 12 varieties of beans cultivated by Aztec farmers, and the legumes are still a mainstay of many meals in southern Mesoamerica and northern South America.

In this recipe, black beans are combined with spinach, cheese, nuts, and spices as a filling for flour tortillas. Although the tortillas are filled and rolled like Tex-Mex/northern Mexico burritos, they are baked and served with red chile sauce, and are to be eaten with a knife and fork.

MAKES 10 LARGE BURRITOS

4 cups cooked black beans (*page 166*), drained,
    or canned black beans, drained and rinsed
3 10-ounce packages frozen chopped spinach,
    thawed and squeezed dry
2 tablespoons minced garlic
1 cup (4 ounces) shredded Monterey Jack cheese
½ cup pine nuts, toasted (*see page 167*)
2 teaspoons ground coriander
1 teaspoon ground cumin
1 teaspoon ají amarillo chile powder
    (*see Ingredients and Sources, page 171*) or cayenne pepper
½ cup chopped fresh cilantro
1⅓ cup fresh lime juice
Salt to taste
1½ cups (7½ ounces) crumbled feta cheese
10 achiote or plain 10-inch flour tortillas
1½ cups Red Chile Sauce (*page 135*)

Preheat the oven to 350°F. Lightly coat the bottom of a 9 x 13 inch baking dish with canola oil. In a large bowl, combine the beans, spinach, garlic, Jack cheese, pine nuts, coriander, cumin, ají powder or cayenne, cilantro, lime juice, and salt. Toss to blend. Add the feta cheese and toss again.

Place 1 cup of the mixture in the center of a tortilla; fold up one-third of the end of the tortilla facing you, then fold in the sides and roll up the tortilla. Repeat with the remaining tortillas and filling. Place in the oiled dish, and bake, uncovered, for 10 to 15 minutes, or until heated through. Remove from the oven, top with the red chile sauce, and serve at once.

Refried Bean and Corn Enchiladas

This recipe incorporates most of the staple foods of pre-Contact Mesoamerica: corn, beans, chiles, and tomatoes. Corn and beans were the foundation of most Aztec and Maya meals, while tomatoes and chiles were most often combined in sauces. Native Mesoamerican cooks probably would have recognized at least three of these foods, but they would have been more familiar with the green, husked tomatoes known as tomatillos than with the larger, red tomato varieties that prevail today.

Makes 8 enchiladas

Sauce

2 tablespoons corn or canola oil
1 cup chopped tomato
½ cup diced onion
2 tablespoons minced garlic
2 teaspoons seeded and minced serrano chile
 (*see Ingredients and Sources, page 171*)
1½ cups homemade vegetable stock (*page 165*), canned low-sodium vegetable stock, or canned low-sodium chicken stock
1 cup minced fresh cilantro
Salt and freshly ground pepper to taste

Enchiladas

8 ears corn, husked
2 cups Refried Beans (*page 125*)
1 cup (4 ounces) shredded Monterey Jack cheese
½ cup coarsely chopped fresh tomato
⅓ cup chopped fresh cilantro
3 tablespoons minced garlic
Salt and freshly ground pepper to taste
Corn or canola oil for pan-frying
8 corn tortillas

For the sauce: In a heavy, medium saucepan, heat the oil over medium heat and sauté the tomato, onion, garlic, and chile until soft, about 8 minutes. Add the stock, cilantro, salt, and pepper. In a blender, puree the mixture in batches until smooth. Return to the pan, place over medium heat, and simmer until lightly thickened, 10 to 15 minutes. Set aside and keep warm.

For the enchiladas: Preheat the oven to 350°F. Place the ears of corn directly on the oven rack and roast for 8 to 10 minutes, or until beginning to color. Remove from the oven and let cool to the touch. Cut the kernels from the corncobs and transfer to a medium bowl. Add the refried beans, cheese, tomato, cilantro, garlic, salt, and pepper.

In a medium skillet, heat ¼ inch oil over medium heat just until shimmering (be careful not to let the oil get too hot, or the tortillas will become too crisp to roll around the filling). Add a tortilla to the oil and cook on both sides until limp, about 45 seconds. Using tongs, transfer the tortilla to a paper towel–lined plate to drain briefly. Spoon 2 to 3 tablespoons of filling in a line down the center of the tortilla, then roll it up. Place seam-side down in a 9 x 13 inch baking dish. Repeat with the remaining tortillas and filling.

Bake, uncovered, for 30 to 35 minutes, or until lightly browned. Remove from the oven. Serve topped with the sauce.

Q'eqchi' Maya corn of different colors, saved for seeds, 2003. Alta Verapaz, Guatemala.
© *Smithsonian Institution*

POTATO AND PINTO BEAN ENCHILADAS

Pre-Contact Mesoamericans considered chiles to be an essential part of every meal, and one of the most common ways of religious fasting was to deny oneself salt and chile with food. Traces of the wild chiles from which most present-day varieties descend have been found at sites in Mexico's Tehuacán Valley dating from 7200 to 5200 BC.

In this recipe, roasted poblanos—large, fleshy, triangle-shaped chiles that are almost always roasted and peeled—add their rich, smoky taste to a filling of cheese, beans, and potatoes, and the enchiladas are topped with Mole Verde (*page 134*).

MAKES 8 TO 10 ENCHILADAS

3 pounds Yukon Gold potatoes, peeled and cut into ½-inch dice
1 cup cooked pinto beans (*page 167*), drained,
    or canned pinto beans, drained and rinsed
2 poblano chiles (*see Ingredients and Sources, page 171*), roasted, peeled,
    seeded, and cut into ¼-inch-wide strips (*see page 167*)
1 to 1½ cups (4 to 6 ounces) shredded Monterey Jack cheese
1 cup chopped fresh cilantro
¼ cup fresh lime juice
Salt and freshly ground pepper to taste
Corn or canola oil for frying
8 to 10 corn tortillas
2 cups Mole Verde (*page 134*)

Preheat the oven to 350°F. Put the potatoes in a large saucepan of salted cold water to cover, bring to a boil, and cook for 5 minutes. Remove from the heat, drain, and set aside to cool. In a medium bowl, combine the potatoes, beans, chiles, cheese, cilantro, and lime juice. Toss to mix. Season with salt and pepper.

In a medium skillet, heat ¼ inch oil over medium heat just until shimmering (be careful not to let the oil get too hot, or the tortillas will become too crisp to roll around the filling). Add a tortilla to the oil and cook on both sides until limp, about 45 seconds. Transfer the tortilla to a paper towel–lined plate to drain briefly. Spoon about 3 heaping tablespoonfuls of filling in a line down the center of the tortilla, then roll it up. Place seam-side down in a 9 x 13 inch baking dish. Repeat to use the remaining tortillas and filling.

Bake, covered, for 15 to 20 minutes, or until heated through. Remove from the oven and place 2 enchiladas on each plate. Top with the sauce and serve.

Chicken Tamales
with Spicy Peanut Sauce

Ten years after the Spanish conquest of present-day Mexico City, Franciscan friar Bernardino de Sahagún was learning the Nahuatl language, interviewing indigenous people about their daily lives, and compiling lists of Aztec foods and dishes. This description of an urban food stall shows how essential tamales had become to the Aztec diet. "[He sells] salted wide tamales, pointed tamales, white tamales, fasting foods, roll-shaped tamales, tamales bound up on top … crumbled, pounded tamales, spotted tamales … white fruit tamales, red fruit tamales, turkey egg tamales, turkey eggs with grains of maize, brick-shaped tamales, braised ones; plain tamales, honey tamales, bee tamales, tamales with grains of maize, squash tamales, crumbled tamales, maize flower tamales. …" While the recipe here calls only for a chicken filling, the technique of folding a masa-lined corn husk around another food would have been well known to Aztec cooks 500 years ago.

Makes 12 tamales

Filling
2 pounds chicken thighs
2 yellow onions, sliced
1 cup chopped fresh cilantro
¼ cup fresh lime juice
¼ cup fresh lemon juice
2 jalapeño chiles, halved, seeded, and sliced
Salt and freshly ground pepper to taste
14 dried corn husks

Masa
½ cup diced onion
½ cup chopped green bell pepper
2 tomatoes, chopped
About 8 cups homemade vegetable stock (*page 165*), canned low-sodium vegetable stock, or canned low-sodium chicken stock
4 cups masa harina

Spicy Peanut Sauce
2 cups Peanut Soup (*page 28*)
½ cup heavy cream

For the filling: Preheat the oven to 350°F. In a Dutch oven or heavy casserole, combine the chicken, onions, ½ cup of the cilantro, lime and lemon juices, chiles, salt, and pepper. Cover and bake until fork-tender, about 2 hours. Remove from the oven. Using a slotted spoon, transfer the chicken and vegetables to a platter, reserving the cooking liquid. Let the chicken cool to the touch. Remove the chicken from the bones and cut the meat into bite-sized pieces. Season to taste with salt and pepper. Put the chicken in a bowl and add the remaining cilantro. Toss to mix. Set aside.

Soak the corn husks in hot water for 30 minutes. Drain and pat dry. Tear 2 of the husks into 12 lengthwise strips.

For the masa: In a blender, puree the onion, bell pepper, and tomato. Add enough vegetable or chicken stock to the liquid reserved from the baked chicken to total 8 cups. In a stockpot, combine the stock mixture and the pureed onion mixture. Bring to a boil over high heat. Gradually whisk in the masa. Reduce heat to low and cook, stirring constantly, for about 15 minutes, or until very thick. Remove from the heat and let cool for about 15 minutes.

Lay a corn husk on a work surface and place about ⅓ cup masa in the center. Spread the masa into a rectangle about 2½ inches wide and 3 inches long, leaving a 1½-inch border on the sides and one end of the husk. Place 2 tablespoons of the chicken mixture in the center of the masa. Fold in the sides of the corn husk. Fold the pointed end of the husk over and fold the broader end over that. Tie the tamale closed crosswise with a strip of husk. Repeat with the remaining corn husks, masa, and chicken mixture. Refrigerate for at least 30 minutes, or up to 2 days.

Bring 1 cup of water to a brisk simmer in a six-quart saucepan or stockpot containing a steamer basket. Place the tamales standing in the steamer basket; cover and cook for 15 to 20 minutes, or until heated through.

Meanwhile, make the sauce: In a small saucepan, combine the soup and cream. Bring to a simmer over medium heat. Remove from the heat and keep warm.

To serve, remove the tamales from the steamer and place on a platter. Open the top of each tamale and pour about 3 tablespoons of the sauce inside. Serve at once.

SALMON CAKES

In many Native communities along the North Pacific Coast, salmon are considered spirit beings that live underneath the sea, traveling up the rivers every summer in the form of fish to provide food for humans. The salmon's annual reappearance prompts one of the most important ceremonies of the year. In the region surrounding present-day Seattle and Vancouver, each Coast Salish community cooked and cleaned the first catch in its own way, sharing the fish with everyone in the village and carefully returning the bones to the water. The people believe that treating the first salmon with respect and expressing gratitude for its return ensures a plentiful supply for the rest of the season.

These savory cakes are bound with egg, mayonnaise, and bread crumbs, and flavored with horseradish, chives, and cayenne. Serve them as a main course or as sandwiches.

Edward S. Curtis (1868–1952). Wishram Fishing Platform, *ca. 1910. Courtesy of the Library of Congress.*

MAKES 4 CAKES

> ½ cup mayonnaise
> 1 tablespoon Dijon mustard
> ¼ cup sour cream
> 1 large egg, lightly beaten
> ½ teaspoon cayenne pepper
> 1 pound salmon fillets, pin bones removed
> ½ cup dried bread crumbs
> ¼ cup prepared horseradish sauce
> ¼ cup minced fresh chives
> ¼ cup unsalted butter, melted
> Salt and freshly ground pepper to taste

In a small bowl, combine the mayonnaise, mustard, sour cream, egg, and cayenne.

Preheat the oven to 350°F. Place the salmon fillets on a baking pan and roast for 10 to 12 minutes, or until just opaque throughout. Transfer to a plate and let cool completely. Remove the skin and crumble the salmon.

In a medium bowl, combine the crumbled salmon, bread crumbs, horseradish, and chives. Stir in the mayonnaise mixture until blended. Season with salt and pepper. Form into 4 firm cakes.

In a large skillet, melt the butter over medium heat and fry the salmon cakes for 4 to 5 minutes on each side, or until golden brown.

Serve the salmon cakes as a main course, with lemon wedges, or in sandwiches, on soft rolls spread with mayonnaise and topped with lettuce.

Cedar-Planked
Fire-Roasted Salmon

Cedar-Planked Fire-Roasted Salmon

This salmon is roasted in the oven, but the planking technique recalls the many ways that North Pacific Coast cooks grill fresh salmon: on poles or racks over a hot fire to eat immediately or by smoking the fish over a slow fire to preserve it for the winter months. In southeast Alaska's Tlingit villages, many backyards feature a smokehouse, which in the summer may be filled with strips of freshly caught salmon hanging on racks over a smoky alder fire for several days until dry.

The sweet-sour taste of the berry glaze in this recipe is just the right counterpoint to the delicate flavor of the fish. Use untreated cedar, cut to size, or purchase a cedar plank from a kitchenware store.

Serves 4 to 6

Berry Glaze

¼ cup fresh or frozen huckleberries
(*see Ingredients and Sources, page 171*) or blueberries
¼ cup fresh or frozen blueberries
¼ cup fresh or frozen raspberries
¼ cup fresh or frozen blackberries
2 to 3 tablespoons water
2 tablespoons sugar

Salmon

¼ cup dried juniper berries (*see Ingredients and Sources, page 171*)
1 to 2 teaspoons salt
1 3-pound salmon fillet, preferably wild Pacific salmon, pin bones removed

Soak a 12-inch cedar plank in water to cover for at least 6 hours; drain.

For the berry glaze: In a medium saucepan, combine all the ingredients for the glaze and bring to a boil over medium heat. Reduce the heat to low and cook, stirring occasionally, for about 8 minutes, or until thickened. Remove from the heat and set aside.

For the salmon: Preheat the oven to 400°F. In a spice grinder or mortar, grind the juniper berries to a powder. Empty into a small bowl and add the salt; stir to blend. Rub the mixture evenly over the flesh side of the salmon. Place the salmon on the drained plank, skin side down, and bake for 8 minutes.

Remove from the oven, leaving the oven on, and brush the berry glaze evenly over the fillet. Return to the oven and bake for another 8 to 10 minutes, or until the salmon is just slightly translucent in the center. Remove from the oven and serve on the plank, if desired, with extra glaze alongside.

Roasted Maple-Brined Turkey Breast

ROASTED MAPLE-BRINED TURKEY BREAST
WITH CRABAPPLE AND CRANBERRY RELISH

Turkey is indigenous to the Americas, but as soon as Europeans "discovered" it, they quickly adopted it as banquet food. Eventually, it supplanted the goose as the centerpiece of holiday meals. Although turkey has become the focus of an entire holiday in the United States, the wild variety was everyday fare for pre-Contact peoples in both North America and Mesoamerica. For the Maya, turkey blood, broth, and cooked meat were essential to ceremonies for healing sicknesses, planting, and praying for rain.

This turkey breast is brined in a mixture flavored with maple syrup, allspice, and sage, then roasted with a baste of maple syrup and butter.

SERVES 6

Maple Brine
 1½ cups maple syrup
 1 cup kosher salt
 1 cup sugar
 6 fresh sage leaves
 4 fresh thyme sprigs
 3 bay leaves
 8 cloves
 1 teaspoon crushed dried juniper berries
  (*see Ingredients and Sources, page 171*)
 1 teaspoon cracked black peppercorns
 1 tablespoon allspice berries
 8 cups water
 4 cups ice cubes

Turkey
 1 6-pound organic bone-in single turkey breast
  or 1 2- to 3-pound boneless turkey breast
 3 tablespoons unsalted butter at room temperature
 Salt and freshly ground pepper to taste

Maple Butter Baste
 ¼ cup unsalted butter
 ¼ cup maple syrup

Crabapple and Cranberry Relish (recipe follows) for serving (optional)

In a large, nonreactive stockpot, combine all the brine ingredients except the ice. Stir to dissolve the salt and sugar. Bring to a boil over high heat and cook for 3 minutes. Remove from the heat, add the ice, and set aside to cool to room temperature. Add the turkey breast, cover, and refrigerate for at least 2 days, or up to 3 days.

Preheat the oven to 325°F. Remove the turkey breast from the refrigerator and the brine. Rinse, pat dry, and rub with the butter, both under and on top of the skin. Season on both sides with salt and pepper. Place the turkey breast on a rack in a roasting pan and roast 2 to 2½ hours for a bone-in breast or 30 to 45 minutes for a boneless breast.

Meanwhile, for the maple butter baste, melt the butter over low heat in a small saucepan. Add the maple syrup and increase the heat to high. Bring to a rolling boil and remove from the heat.

Cook the turkey for about 15 minutes longer, basting with the maple butter every 5 minutes. The turkey is done when an instant-read thermometer inserted into the center of the breast and not touching bone registers 150 to 165°F (150°F will provide juicier white meat). Remove from the oven and transfer to a carving board. Tent with aluminum foil and let stand for 10 minutes. Carve the turkey breast and serve with the relish, if desired.

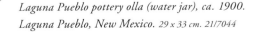

Laguna Pueblo pottery olla (water jar), ca. 1900.
Laguna Pueblo, New Mexico. 29 x 33 cm. 21/7044

CRABAPPLE AND CRANBERRY RELISH

Crabapple is the name given to any species, cultivated or wild, of small, sour apples that are native to many parts of the world. Along the North Pacific Coast, crabapples were steamed before being mashed or combined with dried berries and served on special occasions with oolichan (candlefish) oil. Kwakw<u>a</u>ka'wakw (Kwakiutl) chiefs sometimes held formal crabapple feasts, displaying cedar boxes of crabapples and oolichan oil as a sign of wealth.

MAKES ABOUT 2 CUPS

8 ounces unpeeled crabapples
    or Granny Smith apples, cored and diced
1 cup fresh or frozen cranberries
½ cup sugar, plus more to taste
¼ cup cranberry juice

In a nonreactive saucepan, cook the crabapples or apples over medium heat until soft, 8 to 10 minutes. Add the cranberries and cook until they start to release their liquid, 8 to 10 minutes. Add the ½ cup sugar and stir to dissolve. Add the cranberry juice. Taste and add more sugar if necessary. Use immediately, or cover and refrigerate for up to 3 days.

Kwakw<u>a</u>ka'wakw (Kwakiutl) carved and painted luk'wa (house dish), in the form of a wolf, ca. 1850. Vancouver Island, British Columbia. Red cedar and pigment, 226 x 22 x 88.2 cm. 11/5239

Herb-Roasted Duck Legs with Raspberry Glaze

Native women along the North Pacific Coast have traditionally gathered in groups to pick the berries that ripen in July and August. From strawberries to huckleberries to blueberries to an orange raspberry called a salmonberry, the fruit ripens abundantly and all at once, so Native cooks have developed many ways to preserve it. Without refrigeration or a dehydrator, a Native cook might have placed layers of fresh berries and hot stones in a cedar cooking box. After the cooked berries thickened, she would form them into cakes, which were dried on racks over a fire.

Serves 4

Duck
- ¼ cup canola oil
- Leaves from 1 fresh thyme sprig
- Leaves from 1 fresh rosemary sprig
- 2 garlic cloves, minced
- 8 whole duck legs
- Salt and freshly ground pepper to taste

Raspberry Glaze
- 1 cup fresh or frozen raspberries
- ¼ cup water
- 3 tablespoons sugar

Preheat the oven to 300°F. In a roasting pan, combine the oil, thyme, rosemary, and garlic. Stir to blend. Add the duck legs and turn them to coat with the mixture. Sprinkle on both sides with salt and pepper. Cover with aluminum foil and roast for 1½ hours. Remove from the oven. Increase the oven temperature to 350°F.

Meanwhile, for the raspberry glaze, combine all the glaze ingredients in a medium saucepan and bring to a boil over medium heat. Cook until the sugar is dissolved and the sauce is slightly thickened, about 10 minutes. In a blender, puree the mixture until smooth.

Place the duck legs on a rimmed baking sheet and brush with the glaze. Roast in the oven, uncovered, until crisp, 15 to 20 minutes. Remove from the oven and serve immediately.

Roasted Venison

ROASTED VENISON

Deer and antelope have for millennia been among the most abundant game animals in North America and Mesoamerica. These animals have many uses, both practical and spiritual. The meat can be grilled, fried, stewed, or roasted. Deer hide can be tanned and sewn into soft clothing, robes, and moccasins. And as a symbol of beauty, strength, and bravery, deer have become central to certain dances and ceremonies. The Pueblo tribes of the Southwest incorporate deer and antelope into their winter dances, and the Hupa of northern California perform a 10-day White Deerskin Ceremony to dissipate evil.

Here is a simple recipe for venison roast grilled with fresh herbs.

SERVES 6 TO 8

> ⅓ cup canola oil
> 2 tablespoons minced fresh thyme
> ¼ cup minced fresh basil
> 2 tablespoons minced fresh rosemary
> 1 teaspoon minced garlic
> 1 1-pound boneless venison leg roast
>   (*see Ingredients and Sources, page 171*)
> Salt and freshly ground pepper to taste

In a bowl large enough to hold the venison, combine the oil, herbs, and garlic. Stir to blend. Place the venison in the bowl and turn to coat it on all sides. Let stand at room temperature for at least 30 minutes or up to 1 hour, turning once or twice.

Meanwhile, prepare a hot fire in a charcoal grill, or preheat a gas grill to high. Remove the venison from the bowl and season with salt and pepper. Grill the venison for 15 to 20 minutes on each side, or until an instant-read thermometer inserted in the center of the roast registers 130°F for medium-rare.

Transfer the meat to a carving board, tent with aluminum foil, and let rest for 5 minutes. Cut into thin slices against the grain and serve.

BUFFALO FLANK STEAK

On the Great Plains, Native cooks combined dried buffalo meat with berries and fat to make a long-lasting travel food called pemmican. Carried by hunters and warriors, or eaten any time that fresh meat was difficult to find, pemmican provided a protein-rich, balanced snack. Here, berries and buffalo are combined in a completely different dish, but the basic flavors would have been familiar many centuries ago to Lakota, Cheyenne, Crow, and most other Plains people.

Lakota quilled baby cap, ca. 1900. North Dakota or South Dakota.
1/3337

SERVES 4

Buffalo
⅓ cup corn or canola oil
2 tablespoons minced fresh thyme
¼ cup minced fresh flat-leaf parsley
2 tablespoons minced fresh rosemary
¼ cup minced garlic (8 to 10 cloves)
¼ cup minced shallots
1½ pounds buffalo flank steak (*see Ingredients and Sources, page 171*)
Salt and freshly ground pepper to taste

Caramelized Onions with Blueberries
¼ cup unsalted butter
5 white onions, cut into ½-inch-thick slices
½ cup cider vinegar
1 cup packed brown sugar
2 cups fresh or frozen blueberries
Salt and freshly ground pepper to taste

In a large bowl, combine the oil, herbs, garlic, and shallots. Stir to mix. Add the steak and turn to coat. Cover and refrigerate for at least 6 hours or up to 24 hours, turning once or twice.

Remove the steak from the refrigerator and the bowl. Season with salt and pepper. Light a hot fire in a charcoal grill or preheat a gas grill to high.

Meanwhile, make the onions. In a large, heavy skillet, melt the butter over medium heat. Add the onions and cook, stirring occasionally, until golden brown, 20 to 30 minutes. Add the vinegar and stir to scrape up the browned bits on the bottom of the pan. Stir in the brown sugar and cook, stirring frequently, until thickened, 8 to 10 minutes. Stir in the blueberries and remove from the heat. Season with salt and pepper. Set aside.

Place the steak on the grill and cook for 2 minutes on each side for medium-rare. Transfer to a carving board, tent with aluminum foil, and let rest for 4 minutes. Reheat the onions over low heat. Cut the steak into thin slices against the grain and top with the onions.

John Puzzo. Food stand at the Rosebud Fairgrounds on the Rosebud (Sicangu Lakota) Reservation, South Dakota, 1987. P25252

A Pepperbelly, a non-Native dish sometimes known as a Frito Pie, consists of corn chips topped with cheese, chili, and condiments, served in a bowl or straight from the corn chip bag.

Side Dishes

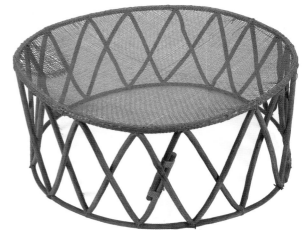

John K. Hillers (1843–1925). An unidentified woman and child sit in front of an adobe house with pumpkins growing in the foreground, ca. 1879. Zuni Pueblo, New Mexico. P23261

Macaguaje (Majaguaje) drying rack for manioc flour, ca. 1935–1948. Rio Caquetá, Colombia. Looped and tied wood, cordage. 21/1778

OYSTER PUDDING

Oysters, clams, and mussels were staple foods for Native coastal tribes, especially along the Atlantic from present-day Canada to the Gulf of Mexico. With many regional varieties and abundant harvests, oysters were incorporated into broths and stews as well as smoked and roasted.

In this recipe, the European ingredients of bread, eggs, and cream are mixed with oysters to make a savory pudding.

SERVES 4 TO 6

1 cup shucked raw oysters with their liquor
¼ cup canola oil
¼ cup chopped leek (white part only)
2 tablespoons minced garlic
3 cups cubed day-old bread
2 tablespoons minced fresh thyme
2 tablespoons minced fresh chervil
2 tablespoons minced fresh flat-leaf parsley
8 large eggs
2 cups heavy cream
Salt and freshly ground pepper to taste

Preheat the oven to 350°F. Butter a 9 x 13 inch baking dish or a 10-inch glass pie plate.

In a small saucepan, heat the oysters and their liquor over medium heat just until the edges curl, about 2 minutes. Remove from the heat and set aside.

In a small skillet, heat the oil over medium heat and sauté the leek and garlic until soft, about 5 minutes. Remove from the heat.

In a medium bowl, combine the bread and herbs. Add the leek mixture. Add the oysters and their liquor. In a small bowl, whisk the eggs and cream together. Pour over the oyster mixture. Toss until well blended and the liquid is absorbed by the bread. Season with salt and pepper.

Spread the mixture in the prepared dish and bake for 30 to 40 minutes, or until the center is firm and a toothpick inserted in the center comes out clean.

Remove from the oven and let cool for 5 minutes. Cut into squares or wedges to serve.

CORN ON THE COB
WITH TOASTED HAZELNUTS

Hazelnuts were a common food for the Native people of the Northeast and Great Lakes, where the nut grows wild on trees and bushes. As the winter progressed and other foods became scarce, hunting tribes depended increasingly on stored nuts and nut flours as a source of protein. In this simple recipe, hazelnuts are ground, mixed with butter, and used to flavor grill-roasted corn.

MAKES 4 EARS

½ cup hazelnuts, toasted and skinned (*see page 167*)
1 cup (2 sticks) unsalted butter at room temperature
4 unhusked ears corn
Salt and freshly ground pepper to taste

Light a hot fire in a charcoal grill, or preheat a gas grill to high.

In a food processor, pulse the nuts 5 or 6 times until coarsely ground. Add the butter and process until combined, about 15 seconds. Scoop into a small bowl.

Peel back the corn husks and remove the silk. Brush the corn lightly with the hazelnut butter and reserve the remaining butter. Fold the husks back down over the corn and tie them closed with a strip of husk. Grill the corn, turning to cook on all sides, for 6 to 8 minutes, or until evenly charred. Transfer to plates and serve in the husks with the remaining hazelnut butter and salt and pepper alongside.

Hazelnut and Honey–Roasted Acorn Squash

Hazelnut and Honey–Roasted Acorn Squash

Like the recipe for Corn on the Cob on page 111, this recipe combines two of the staple foods of the Northeast's Haudenosaunee (Iroquois) and Algonquin peoples. So integrated were squash and nuts into the woodland cultures that several tribes named their seasons or months for them. For example, the Wampanoag word for *summer* is *Mat-terll-a-waw-kees-wush*, which means literally "squash ripe, beans edible."

Here, slices of acorn squash are spread with a hazelnut-honey butter and roasted until tender.

Serves 4

½ cup hazelnuts, toasted and skinned (*see page 167*)
½ cup (1 stick) unsalted butter at room temperature
2 tablespoons honey
2 medium to large acorn squash, unpeeled, seeded, and cut into 1-inch-thick wedges
Salt and freshly ground pepper to taste

Preheat the oven to 350°F.

In a food processor, pulse the nuts 5 to 6 times, or until coarsely ground. Add the butter and process for 15 to 20 seconds, or until combined. Scrape into a medium bowl. Add the honey and whisk until smooth.

Oil a rimmed baking sheet. Arrange the squash wedges, skin side down, on the prepared pan. Sprinkle with salt and pepper and spread with the hazelnut butter. Roast for 30 minutes, or until fork-tender. Remove from the oven and serve hot.

Maniwaki Algonquin (River Desert) birch bark box etched with maple leaves and stars, 1920–1925. Between Désert and Gatineau rivers, Quebec, Canada. 15/9458

SAUTÉED GREENS WITH BACON

Many Native gatherers and cooks developed an intimate knowledge of the culinary and medicinal properties of the wild greens that flourished around them. Along the North Pacific Coast, the first green shoots of spring—wild celery, purple clover, dandelion greens, wild spinach, and watercress—broke the tedium of a winter diet of dried fish and fish oil. Although the greens in this dish are cultivated, wild counterparts to the arugula and mustard greens still grow in the inland mountains and valleys that surround the Columbia River Gorge in Washington and Oregon.

Here, the greens are sautéed with bacon, leek, and scallions, then brightened with cider vinegar.

SERVES 4 TO 6

8 ounces slab or thick-sliced bacon, cut into 1-inch cubes or squares
8 ounces collard greens, stemmed, cut into 2-inch pieces, and well rinsed (about 2½ cups)
8 ounces mustard greens, dandelion greens, beet greens, or kale, stemmed, cut into 2-inch pieces, and well rinsed (about 2½ cups) (*see Ingredients and Sources, page 171*)
8 ounces arugula, cut into 2-inch pieces and well rinsed (about 2½ cups)
1 large leek, white part only, cut into 2-inch pieces and well rinsed (about 1 cup)
1 bunch scallions, green parts only, cut into 2-inch pieces (about 1 cup)
½ cup cider vinegar
2 cups water
Salt and freshly ground pepper to taste

In a large, heavy saucepan, sauté the bacon over medium heat until just crisp. Pour off all but 2 tablespoons of the fat. Add the three kinds of greens, the leek, and the scallions. Reduce the heat to low, cover, and cook until wilted, about 10 minutes. Add the vinegar, water, salt, and pepper. Uncover and cook, stirring occasionally, for 8 to 10 minutes, or until the greens are tender. Serve warm.

POTATO AND HORSERADISH PUREE

Hundreds of varieties of potatoes flourished in South America as early as 4,000 years ago, but the tuber was received with suspicion in Europe when explorers first returned with samples in the 1500s. Although pre-Inka and Inka farmers had developed varieties of potatoes suited to every climate, from tropical to high-altitude, the potato's agricultural and culinary possibilities were slow to be recognized on other continents. In North America, the potato was completely unknown (although Native communities in the Southeast grew sweet potatoes extensively) until Irish immigrants introduced it in 1719. Its popularity, however, has steadily increased ever since.

For this side dish, Yukon Golds are pureed with cream, butter, and horseradish root to make a spicy golden version of mashed potatoes.

SERVES 4 TO 6

> 1 pound Yukon Gold potatoes, peeled and halved
> 1 2½-inch piece horseradish root
> ¼ cup heavy cream
> 3 tablespoons unsalted butter
> Salt and freshly ground pepper to taste

Put the potatoes in a medium saucepan of salted cold water and bring to a boil; reduce the heat to a brisk simmer and cook until fork-tender, 20 to 25 minutes. Drain, then place in a medium bowl and keep warm.

Meanwhile, in a small saucepan of boiling water, cook the horseradish root for 5 to 7 minutes; drain. Repeat twice, using fresh water each time. Add to the potatoes and set aside to keep warm.

In a small saucepan, combine the cream and butter. Cook over low heat until the butter is melted.

Using an electric mixer, puree the potatoes and horseradish. Gradually beat in the cream mixture to make a soft puree. Season to taste with salt and pepper and serve at once.

YUCA
WITH GARLIC AND BUTTER

Not to be confused with the yucca cactus that grows in the Desert Southwest, yuca root in its bitter and sweet forms is a starchy tuber native to the tropical regions of Mesoamerica and South America. It is also known as manioc or cassava. Some researchers believe that Native Amazonians were cultivating the bitter version of yuca root more than 3,500 years ago—and devising ways of soaking and heating the tubers to remove their highly poisonous chemicals. Bitter yuca has been developed into many different products: tapioca is the most internationally recognized, but the most important is probably manioc flour, which can be made into a bread that is still eaten every day throughout the Amazon Basin and the tropical areas of Venezuela and Colombia.

In this simple recipe, sweet yuca is baked with butter, garlic, and chives as a side dish to serve with roasted or grilled meats.

SERVES 6 TO 8

3 pounds yuca (*see Ingredients and Sources, page 171*), peeled, cut into 1-inch wedges, and fibrous veins removed
1 cup (2 sticks) unsalted butter, melted
¼ cup minced garlic (8 to 10 cloves)
Salt and freshly ground pepper to taste
¼ cup minced fresh chives

Preheat the oven to 300°F. Butter a 9 x 13 inch baking dish.

In a large pot of salted boiling water, cook the yuca until tender, 6 to 8 minutes. Drain and let cool slightly.

Put the yuca in the prepared dish. In a small bowl, combine the butter and garlic. Pour over the yuca and season with salt and pepper. Cover the dish with aluminum foil and bake for 45 minutes, or until very tender.

Remove from the oven, transfer to a serving bowl, and sprinkle with chives.

A. Hyatt Verrill (1871–1954).
A Patamona girl grinds manioc
(yuca) into a hollowed-out log,
1917. Mazaruni River headwaters,
Guyana. P00252

SUCCOTASH

This dish of beans and corn, originally called *m'sickqquatasch* in the Narragansett language, was well known to Haudenosaunee (Iroquois) and Algonquin cooks, who introduced it to the earliest English settlers. This version uses roasted corn kernels, fava beans, and cranberry beans flavored with fresh marjoram. Walnut oil replaces the bear fat called for in some traditional recipes.

SERVES 6

6 ears corn, husked, or 3 cups frozen corn kernels, thawed
1 pound fresh fava or lima beans, shelled,
    or 2 cups frozen fava or lima beans
4 cups cooked cranberry beans (*page 166*),
    plus ¼ cup bean cooking liquid
¼ cup finely diced red onion
1 large tomato, diced
2 tablespoons walnut oil
2 tablespoons sherry vinegar
2 tablespoons minced fresh marjoram
Pinch of cayenne pepper
Salt and freshly ground pepper to taste

Preheat the oven to 350°F. If using fresh corn, place the ears directly on the oven rack. If using frozen corn, spread the thawed kernels on a rimmed baking sheet and pat dry with paper towels. Roast for 8 to 10 minutes, or until they begin to color. Remove from the oven and let cool to the touch. If using fresh corn, cut the kernels from the ears. Set aside.

If using fresh fava beans, blanch them in a medium saucepan of salted boiling water for 2 minutes. Remove from the heat, drain, and plunge into a bowl of cold water. Skin the beans by pinching each to remove the skin. If using frozen fava beans, you may skip this step.

In a saucepan of salted boiling water, cook the fava or lima beans until tender, 3 to 4 minutes. Drain.

In a medium bowl, combine the roasted corn kernels, fava or lima beans, cranberry beans, cranberry bean broth, onion, tomato, oil, and vinegar. Toss to mix. Add the marjoram, cayenne, salt, and pepper. Toss again and serve.

HONEY-ROASTED RUTABAGAS

Rutabagas and turnips are both members of the cabbage family, and in Europe the rutabaga is sometimes referred to as the Swedish turnip. Although rutabagas were introduced to the Americas by northern Europeans, Plains tribes harvested at least two varieties of wild turnips (part of a different vegetable family), which are called *tinpsila* in the Dakota language. The long, tender-skinned variety is called *sahiyela tinpsila*, or "Cheyenne turnip." Knowledgeable Native cooks on the Plains still dig for wild, or prairie, turnips each June, after their purple flowers have blossomed.

Cubed and roasted with butter and honey, rutabagas here become a golden-brown accompaniment to roasted meat or poultry.

SERVES 4 TO 6

3 pounds rutabagas, peeled and cut into 1½-inch cubes
½ cup (1 stick) unsalted butter, melted
½ cup honey
Salt and freshly ground pepper to taste

Preheat the oven to 350°F. In a large bowl, combine the rutabagas, butter, and honey. Toss to coat. Season with salt and pepper and toss again.

Spread the mixture in a 9 x 13 inch baking dish and roast until golden brown and fork-tender, 30 to 35 minutes. Remove from the oven and serve hot.

Green Chile Rice

GREEN CHILE RICE

Mixed with Mole Verde (*page 134*), rice takes on a green color and chile flavor and is a great accompaniment to grilled chicken or fish. When served with Frijoles Negros (*page 124*) or Refried Beans (*page 125*), it makes a flavorful and nutritious vegetarian meal.

Serves 4 to 6

1 tablespoon corn or canola oil
¼ cup diced onion
1 to 2 garlic cloves, minced
1½ cups long-grain white rice
2 cups water
1 cup Mole Verde (*page 134*)
Salt and freshly ground pepper to taste

In a large, heavy saucepan, heat the oil over medium heat and sauté the onion and garlic until the onion is translucent, about 3 minutes. Add the rice and sauté until well coated, about 3 minutes. Stir in the water, mole verde, salt, and pepper. Bring to a boil, reduce the heat to low, and cover. Cook for 30 to 35 minutes, or until the liquid is absorbed and the rice is tender.

Fluff the rice with a fork. Taste and adjust the seasoning. Serve hot.

Clockwise from top: Refried Beans, Frijoles Negros, Maple and Molasses Baked Beans

Maple and Molasses Baked Beans

Maple candy was a traditional treat for Native children in the Northeast and Great Lakes regions, but cooks also depended upon maple sugar and syrup to season nearly every kind of fruit, vegetable, grain, and fish. In seasonal sugaring camps near Lake Superior, Ojibwe families tapped the same trees each year, boiling the sap all night over a slow fire and granulating the thickened syrup in wooden troughs. Stored in specially sized birch bark containers called *makuks*, the sugar lasted for months. Although techniques have changed, sugar making still begins in late winter or early spring, when warmer temperatures thaw the sap in sugar maple trees.

In this recipe, maple syrup, molasses, and bacon add a depth of flavor to cooked cranberry beans.

Serves 4 to 6

2 cups dried cranberry beans, rinsed and picked over
4 ounces slab or thick-sliced bacon, cut into
    1-inch cubes or squares
½ cup diced onion
¼ cup dark molasses
½ cup maple syrup
2 tablespoons Dijon mustard
2 tablespoons dry mustard
Salt and freshly ground pepper to taste

In a large saucepan, soak the beans overnight in water to cover by 2 inches.

Drain and add water to cover by 2 inches. Bring to a boil over high heat, then reduce the heat to a simmer and cook, uncovered, until tender, 1 to 1½ hours. Remove from the heat and drain, reserving the liquid.

Preheat the oven to 300°F. In a large, heavy pot, sauté the bacon over medium heat until the fat is rendered and the bacon is lightly browned, 5 to 8 minutes. Add the onion and sauté until translucent, about 3 minutes. Stir in the molasses, maple syrup, and both mustards. Bring to a boil and stir in the beans, along with enough of the reserved bean broth to barely cover the beans without making them soupy. Cover and bake until the beans are well flavored and have absorbed the liquid, 2 to 3 hours. Remove from the oven. Season with salt and pepper and serve.

FRIJOLES NEGROS

Black beans, or *buul*, were and still are a staple Maya food. Scooped up with tortillas, incorporated into maize tamale dough, combined with chiles and toasted squash seeds in a stew, and often flavored with epazote, black beans were available to Maya cooks when meat was scarce. Today in Yucatán and Oaxaca, black bean paste is an integral ingredient in many elaborate regional dishes.

Serve this side dish—flavored with cumin, coriander, and fresh cilantro—with roasted or grilled meats, or alongside enchiladas or tacos.

SERVES 6 TO 8

2 cups dried black beans, rinsed and picked over
1 jalapeño chile, seeded and thinly sliced
1 yellow onion, chopped
2 tablespoons ground cumin
2 tablespoons ground coriander
¼ cup minced garlic (8 to 10 cloves)
Salt and freshly ground pepper to taste
1 cup chopped fresh cilantro

In a large saucepan, soak the beans overnight in water to cover by 2 inches. Drain and add water to cover by 2 inches. Add the chile, onion, cumin, coriander, and garlic. Bring to a boil over high heat, then reduce the heat to a simmer and cook, uncovered, until tender, about 1½ hours. Remove from the heat and let cool in the liquid for about 15 minutes. Season to taste with salt and pepper. Stir in the cilantro and serve.

REFRIED BEANS

SERVES 4 TO 6

Maya and Aztec cooks were very familiar with pinto beans, but before the arrival of Europeans, plant oils and animal fats were relatively scarce, so frying was not a common technique. Refried beans—traditionally made with pork lard—are most certainly a post-Contact dish, but they have become ubiquitous in Mexican and Mexican American cooking.

This dish—seasoned with cumin, coriander, and garlic—can accompany almost any Mexican or southwestern main course.

2 cups dried pinto beans, rinsed and picked over
2 tablespoons corn or canola oil, plus ¾ cup
1 onion, diced
¼ cup minced garlic (8 to 10 cloves)
2 tablespoons ground cumin
2 tablespoons ground coriander
Salt and freshly ground pepper to taste

In a large saucepan, soak the beans overnight in water to cover by 2 inches. Drain and add water to cover by 2 inches.

In a medium skillet, heat the 2 tablespoons oil over medium heat. Add the onion, garlic, cumin, and coriander. Sauté until the onion is translucent, 3 minutes. Add the onion mixture to the beans. Bring to a boil, reduce the heat to a simmer, and cook, uncovered, until tender, about 1½ hours. Drain the beans, reserving the liquid.

Transfer half of the beans to a large bowl and mash with a potato masher or the back of a spoon. Return to the other beans and stir to mix. Add some of the reserved cooking liquid to achieve a thick paste. Season with salt and pepper.

In a large, heavy skillet, heat the ¾ cup oil over medium-high heat. Add the bean mixture and cook, stirring frequently, until heated through. Remove from the heat and serve hot.

Sauces & Salsas

Most people in the United States know that salsa originated in Mexico, but many may not realize just how deeply rooted salsas are in Maya and Aztec cuisines. Pre-Contact cooks invented hundreds of salsas, most of them made from the same vegetables used in their base dishes. Chiles of all kinds, tomatoes, and tomatillos were the most common ingredients, as they are today; onion and citrus juice are European additions. The friar Bernardino de Sahagún, who in the 1500s documented Aztec foods in great detail, described the sauces for sale in an Aztec food market: "He sells … mild red chile sauce, yellow chile sauce, hot chile sauce … sauce of smoked chile, heated [sauces], bean sauce; [he sells] … mushroom sauce, sauce of small squash, sauce of large tomatoes, sauce of ordinary tomatoes, sauce of various kinds of sour herbs, avocado sauce." The list goes on.

Russell Lee. Couple in front of a house with drying chile peppers, 1940. Isleta Pueblo, New Mexico. Courtesy of the Library of Congress.

SALSA FRESCA

The most popular version of salsa is an uncooked mixture of fresh chiles and tomatoes, spiked with cilantro.

MAKES ABOUT 3 CUPS

¼ cup tomato juice
6 tablespoons chopped fresh cilantro
6 tablespoons chopped onion
2 tablespoons seeded and chopped Anaheim chile
    (*see Ingredients and Sources, page 171*)
1 teaspoon seeded and chopped serrano chile
    (*see Ingredients and Sources, page 171*)
1 teaspoon seeded and chopped jalapeño chile
3 to 4 tomatoes, finely diced (3 cups)
¼ cup chopped scallions, including green parts
¼ cup chopped red bell pepper
1 teaspoon minced garlic
½ teaspoon dried oregano, crumbled
2 tablespoons corn or canola oil
1 tablespoon red wine vinegar
Salt and freshly ground pepper to taste

In a blender, combine the tomato juice, ¼ cup cilantro, 2 tablespoons onion, and chiles, and puree until smooth.

In a medium bowl, combine remaining cilantro and onion, tomatoes, scallions, bell pepper, garlic, oregano, oil, and vinegar. Stir in the pureed mixture. Add salt and pepper to taste. Let stand at room temperature for at least 1 hour, or cover and refrigerate for up to 3 days. Serve cold or at room temperature.

Salsa Quemada

Quemada ("burned") refers to the roasted vegetables in this flavorful salsa.

Makes about 4 cups

8 plum (Roma) tomatoes, halved
1 small white onion, peeled and cut into 3 wedges
8 scallions, including green parts,
    trimmed and cut horizontally in half
1 serrano chile, seeded and halved
    (*see Ingredients and Sources, page 171*)
2 garlic cloves, peeled
¼ cup fresh lime juice
2 to 3 tablespoons water (optional)
Salt and freshly ground pepper to taste

Preheat the oven to 450°F. Spread the tomatoes, onion, scallions, chile, and garlic on a rimmed baking sheet. Roast until the tomatoes and onion are well charred, 30 to 40 minutes.

Remove from the oven, transfer the mixture to a blender, and add the lime juice. Puree to a thick salsa, adding water as needed. Stir in the salt and pepper. Taste and adjust the seasoning. Use immediately, or cover and refrigerate for up to 3 days.

Pico de Gallo

An even simpler version of Salsa Fresca, Pico de Gallo takes only minutes to make and is a perfect companion to tortilla chips, tacos, and roasted and grilled meats.

Makes about 3 cups

4 tomatoes, finely diced
1 small white onion, finely diced
¼ cup finely diced red bell pepper
¼ cup seeded and finely diced green Anaheim chile
    (*see Ingredients and Sources, page 171*)
2 teaspoons seeded and minced jalapeño chile
½ cup chopped fresh cilantro
¼ cup fresh lime juice
Salt to taste

In a medium bowl, combine all the ingredients and toss to mix. Taste and adjust the seasoning. Use immediately, or cover and refrigerate for up to 3 days.

Mam Maya woman's woven cotton huipil (shirt), ca. 1980. Concepción Chiquirichapa, Guatemala. 26/2643

ROASTED JALAPEÑO AND TOMATO SALSA

Roasting chiles and peppers brings out their sweet flavor and adds a smoky note to this salsa.

MAKES ABOUT 4 CUPS

3 tomatoes, finely diced
¼ cup finely diced onion
1 jalapeño chile, roasted, peeled, and finely diced (*see page 167*)
¼ red bell pepper, roasted, peeled, and finely diced (*see page 167*)
¼ green Anaheim chile (*see Ingredients and Sources, page 171*),
　　roasted, peeled, and finely diced (*see page167*)
1 tablespoon minced garlic
½ cup chopped fresh cilantro
¼ cup fresh lime juice
Salt to taste

In a medium bowl, combine all the ingredients. Toss to mix. Taste and adjust the seasoning. Use immediately, or cover and refrigerate for up to 3 days.

Tomatillo Salsa

This classic green sauce derives its tangy flavor from roasted tomatillos, mixed with chile, garlic, and cilantro.

Makes about 4 cups

10 to 12 tomatillos, husked, rinsed, and halved
Corn or canola oil for coating, plus 2 tablespoons
1 cup diced onion
2 tablespoons seeded and minced serrano chile
  (*see Ingredients and Sources, page 171*)
1 cup chopped fresh cilantro
2 tablespoons minced garlic
¼ cup fresh lime juice
Salt to taste

Preheat the oven to 350°F. Brush the tomatillos with oil and spread on a rimmed baking sheet. Roast for 8 to 10 minutes, or until soft.

In a blender, combine the roasted tomatillos, 2 tablespoons oil, onion, chile, cilantro, garlic, and lime juice. Puree to make a coarse salsa. Stir in the salt. Taste and adjust the seasoning. Use immediately, or cover and refrigerate for up to 3 days.

BLACK BEAN AND ANCHO CHILE SALSA

Poblanos and ancho chiles (dried poblanos) combine with black beans to make a deeply flavored but mild salsa; add more ancho chile if you would like it hotter.

2 poblano chiles (*see Ingredients and Sources, page 171*), roasted, peeled, seeded, and finely diced (*see page 167*)
2 ancho chiles (*see Ingredients and Sources, page 171*), crumbled
2 cups cooked black beans (*page 166*), drained, or canned black beans, drained and rinsed
3 tomatoes, diced
½ cup diced red onion
2 tablespoons minced garlic
½ cup chopped fresh cilantro
½ cup tomato juice
3 tablespoons lime juice
Salt to taste

In a large bowl, combine all the ingredients and toss to mix. Taste and adjust the seasoning. Use immediately, or cover and refrigerate for up to 3 days.

MOLE VERDE

This complex green sauce from Oaxaca descends from the moles that were made for centuries by Maya people and adopted by the Aztecs. Use it in Chicken and Mole Verde Tacos (*page 78*), to flavor Green Chile Rice (*page 121*), or serve it with poached or grilled chicken or fish.

MAKES ABOUT 3 CUPS

8 to 10 tomatillos, husked, rinsed, and halved
¼ cup corn or canola oil
1 cup chopped white onion
½ cup minced garlic (about 2 heads)
1 poblano chile (*see Ingredients and Sources, page 171*), roasted, peeled, and chopped (*see page 167*)
1 green Anaheim chile (*see Ingredients and Sources, page 171*), roasted, peeled, and chopped (*see page 167*)
1 bunch scallions, including light green parts, chopped
1 cup chopped fresh cilantro leaves
½ cup fresh lime juice
4 cups homemade vegetable stock (*page 165*), canned low-sodium vegetable stock, or canned low-sodium chicken stock
Salt and freshly ground pepper to taste

Preheat the oven to 350°F. Brush the tomatillos with 2 tablespoons of the oil and spread on a rimmed baking sheet. Roast for 10 to 15 minutes, or until soft and lightly browned.

In a large, nonreactive pot, heat the remaining 2 tablespoons oil over medium heat and sauté the onion and garlic until golden brown, 10 to 15 minutes. Add the poblano and Anaheim chiles, the scallions, cilantro, lime juice, and tomatillos. Sauté for 5 to 8 minutes to blend the flavors. Add the stock, salt, and pepper. Bring to a boil, reduce the heat to a simmer, and cook, uncovered, for 40 to 45 minutes, or until reduced by half. Remove from heat and let cool for about 10 minutes. Transfer to a blender and puree in batches until smooth. Taste and adjust the seasoning. Serve warm. To store, let cool, cover, and refrigerate for up to 3 days.

Red Chile Sauce

With many regional versions, red chile sauce is a kitchen basic for cooks in Mesoamerica and the southwestern part of North America. Serve this hearty, rustic sauce with rice, tortillas, eggs, and meats, as well as a topping for dishes such as Baked Black Bean and Spinach Burritos (*page 88*).

Makes about 2 cups

¼ cup corn or canola oil
1 yellow onion, chopped
2 tablespoons crumbled pasilla chile
    (*see Ingredients and Sources, page 171*)
2 tablespoons chopped fresh or crumbled dried red
    New Mexico chile (*see Ingredients and Sources, page 171*)
2 tablespoons crumbled guajillo chile
    (*see Ingredients and Sources, page 171*)
2 cups chicken stock
2 tablespoons ground dried oregano
2 to 3 teaspoons ground cumin
Salt to taste

In a heavy, medium saucepan, heat the oil over medium heat and sauté the onion until translucent, about 3 minutes. Add the three chiles and sauté for 3 to 5 minutes, stirring frequently to prevent burning. Add the stock, oregano, and cumin. Bring to a boil, reduce the heat to a simmer, and cook for 10 minutes.

In a blender, puree the mixture in batches until smooth. Season with salt. Serve warm. To store, let cool, cover, and refrigerate for up to 1 week.

john garcia

Breads

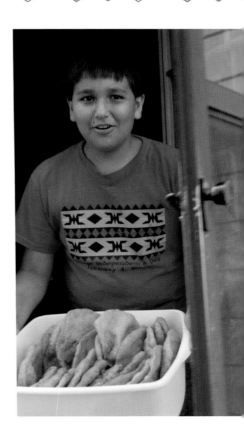

Christopher Cote (Osage) serving fry bread at his grandmother's house during the annual I'n-lon-shka Dances, June 2006. Pawhuska, Oklahoma. © *Smithsonian Institution*

John D. Garcia (K'apovi [Santa Clara Pueblo], b. 1942). Untitled, 2003. Acrylic on paper, 29 x 43.5 cm. 26/3047. In this painting, the six colors of corn represent the cardinal directions and specific animals. The multicolored ear represents Opaa Piye (Sky, in the Tewa language) and the eagle; the white ear, Than Piye (East) and the badger; the red ear, Akon Piye (South) and the bobcat; the yellow ear, Tsan Piye (West) and the black bear; the blue ear, Ping Piye (North) and the mountain lion; and the black ear, Nan Nun (Below) and the mole. The female figures on either side of the corn plant represent the Santa Clara Pueblo's Winter and Summer Clans.

Blue Corn Bread

Blue Corn Bread

A staple throughout the Southwest, blue corn is especially important for traditional Hopi dishes, including paper-thin piki bread. The Hopi are sometimes called "the people of the blue corn." According to the Hopi origin story, when the people emerged into the present world, they were invited to choose from several kinds of corn. The Hopi chose the short blue ear, signifying that life would be difficult but that they would be strong and enduring.

Blue cornmeal adds a dusky flavor and deep color to this bread.

MAKES 8 TO 12 PIECES

1½ cups blue cornmeal (*see Ingredients and Sources, page 171*)
1 cup yellow cornmeal
½ cup sugar
1 teaspoon salt
2 tablespoons baking powder
¾ cup milk
2 large eggs
1 large egg yolk
⅓ cup unsalted butter, melted

Preheat the oven to 350°F. Butter a 9 x 13 inch baking pan.

In a large bowl, combine the blue and yellow cornmeal, sugar, salt, and baking powder. Stir with a whisk to blend. In another large bowl, combine the milk, eggs, egg yolk, and melted butter. Whisk until blended. Pour the wet ingredients into the dry ingredients and stir just until combined; do not overmix.

Pour the batter into the prepared pan and bake until lightly browned, 20 to 25 minutes. Remove from the oven. Cut into squares and serve warm.

Fry Bread

Fry Bread

When reservations were created in the mid-1800s, the U.S. government promised to supply Native people with "commodity" foods to replace the subsistence foods that were no longer available to them. For European Americans, a basic commodity is wheat, so wheat flour became a staple for people whose diets for thousands of years had been based on corn. Over the past 150 years, this change has had many effects on Native American cooking, not the least of which is the invention of fry bread. One of the most popular and delicious (and least healthful) of modern Native foods, fry bread is for many communities both a festival and an everyday food. Recipes and techniques vary, but the result is basically the same: a dough leavened with baking powder and deep-fried until puffed and golden brown.

MAKES 6 ROUND FLAT BREADS

> 2 cups all-purpose flour
> 1 teaspoon baking powder
> 1 teaspoon salt
> 2 tablespoons sugar
> ¾ cup milk, plus more if necessary
> Corn or canola oil for deep-frying
> Sugar mixed with ground cinnamon for topping (optional)

In a medium bowl, combine the flour, baking powder, salt, and the 2 tablespoons sugar. Stir with a whisk to blend. Stir in the ¾ cup milk to make a stiff dough, adding a bit more if necessary. On a lightly floured board, divide the dough into 6 pieces. Form each into a ball, then roll into a disk about ¼ inch thick.

In a Dutch oven or deep fryer, heat 3 inches oil to 350°F on a deep-fat thermometer. Using a sharp knife, cut an X in the center of each dough disk. Place one disk at a time in the hot oil and cook until golden brown, about 2 minutes on each side. Using tongs, transfer to a paper towel–lined plate to drain. Keep warm in a low oven while frying the remaining disks.

Serve at once, either plain or sprinkled with cinnamon sugar.

RED ONION AND HERB FRY BREAD

This nontraditional version
of fry bread, flavored with
red onion and fresh thyme,
parsley, and rosemary, is
a great accompaniment to
Butternut Squash Soup
(*page 25*).

MAKES 6 ROUND FLAT BREADS

1½ cups all-purpose flour
2 teaspoons baking powder
1 teaspoon salt
½ cup milk
1 teaspoon corn or canola oil, plus more for deep-frying
¼ cup finely diced red onion
1 teaspoon minced fresh thyme
1 teaspoon minced fresh flat-leaf parsley
1 teaspoon minced fresh rosemary

In a medium bowl, combine the flour, baking powder, and salt. Stir with
a whisk to blend. In a small saucepan, heat the milk over low heat until
warm. Stir in the 1 teaspoon oil. Gradually stir the milk mixture into the dry
ingredients to make a thick dough. Stir in the onion and herbs until combined.

On a floured board, divide the dough into 6 pieces. Form each into a ball.
Cover the dough balls with a damp towel and let rest for 15 to 20 minutes.
Roll out each ball into a disk about ¼ inch thick. Using a sharp knife, cut
an X in the center of each dough disk.

In a Dutch oven or deep fryer, heat 3 inches oil to 350°F on a deep-fat
thermometer. Fry the dough one piece at a time until golden brown, about 2
minutes on each side. Using tongs, transfer to a paper towel–lined plate to drain.
Keep warm in a low oven while frying the remaining disks. Serve at once.

Variation: Pumpkin Fry Bread
Add 2 tablespoons pumpkin puree and ¼ cup finely diced uncooked
butternut squash to the dough in the above recipe, omitting the onion and
herbs. Dust the hot fry bread with confectioners' sugar or serve with warm
maple syrup.

CORN BREAD

Corn bread as most North Americans know it today was one of the earliest post-Contact foods. Many European settlers in the 1600s and 1700s considered maize inferior to wheat because the American grain, lacking gluten, does not combine with yeast to make bread rise. The newcomers adapted Native recipes for unleavened corn breads, however, by combining maize flour with water and eggs to make cakes that they called variously johnnycakes, hoecakes, ash cakes, or corn pones. The name *corn pone* derives from the Algonquian word *apan*, which means "baked."

MAKES 9 3-INCH SQUARES

> 1 cup cornmeal
> 1 cup all-purpose flour
> 4 teaspoons sugar
> 4 teaspoons baking powder
> ½ teaspoon salt
> 1 cup milk
> 1 large egg
> ¼ cup corn or canola oil

Preheat the oven to 350°F. Butter a 9-inch square baking pan.

In a medium bowl, combine the cornmeal, flour, sugar, baking powder, and salt. Stir with a whisk to blend. In another medium bowl, combine the milk, egg, and oil. Whisk until combined. Stir the wet ingredients into the dry ingredients just until combined; do not overmix.

Pour the batter into the prepared pan and bake for 20 to 25 minutes, or until lightly browned. Remove from the oven. Cut into squares and serve warm.

Desserts

Minnesota Chippewa beaded cotton man's shoulder bag (detail) with a flower, leaf, and blueberry design, 1885–1900. Leech Lake Reservation, Minnesota. 112 x 39 cm. 25/389

INDIAN PUDDING

Pre-Contact versions of this pudding contained cornmeal, dried fruit, nut butter, and water, with maple sugar or honey as a sweetener. After the arrival of Europeans, milk or cream replaced the water, and often eggs, molasses, and more spices were added, as in this recipe, which incorporates dried currants.

SERVES 4 TO 6

3 cups milk, plus ¼ cup
1 cup maple syrup
¼ cup unsalted butter
1½ cups cornmeal
1½ cups dried currants
½ teaspoon ground ginger
¼ teaspoon ground nutmeg

Preheat the oven to 325°F. Butter an 8-inch square baking dish.

In a medium saucepan, combine the 3 cups milk and the maple syrup. Bring to a simmer over medium heat, stirring to mix in the maple syrup. Add the butter and stir until melted.

In a small bowl, combine the cornmeal, currants, ginger, and nutmeg; stir to blend. Stir into the milk mixture and cook, stirring frequently, for 10 minutes; the mixture will thicken to the consistency of mush.

Pour the mixture into the prepared dish and smooth to even the top. Pour the ¼ cup milk on top.

Bake for 30 minutes, or until golden brown. Place large spoonfuls of the pudding in warmed bowls and serve at once.

CHESTNUT PUDDING

American chestnuts, native to the Appalachians, were once widely harvested—and later cultivated—in the Northeast. Native people used the nuts in many ways, both medicinal and culinary. Chestnut tea, made from leaves steeped in hot water, was a Native remedy for whooping cough, and a butter made from chestnut oil was used with corn bread, squash, and other foods. In 1904, however, a blight wiped out nearly all American chestnut trees—those grown in the United States today are most often a Chinese variety.

This pudding of chestnut puree with spices and dried cherries makes a comforting winter dessert.

SERVES 4 TO 6

½ cup unsweetened chestnut puree
  (*see Ingredients and Sources, page 171*)
¾ cup packed brown sugar
3 eggs
2 cups heavy cream
1 tablespoon ground cinnamon
½ teaspoon ground nutmeg
½ cup dried cherries

Preheat the oven to 350°F. Butter an 8-inch square baking dish.

In a medium bowl, combine all the ingredients and stir to mix well. Pour into the prepared dish. Place the dish in a roasting pan and add hot water to the pan to come halfway up the sides of the dish. Bake for 45 to 50 minutes, or until firm to the touch. Remove from the oven. Serve warm.

Cranberry Crumble

CRANBERRY CRUMBLE

English settlers in northeastern North America called them "crane-berries," because the white flowers that appeared in the bogs in early June reminded them of cranes' heads. But to the Wampanoag people of the region, they were known as *sassamenesh*. Growing in wetland areas with sandy soils, the North American cranberry is twice as big as any other variety, and Native cooks have a long history of using both fresh and dried cranberries to flavor many kinds of dishes. Aquinnah Wampanoags on Martha's Vineyard still designate the second Tuesday of October as Cranberry Day: offices are closed, people harvest the berries, elders teach children about cranberrying, and in the evening Native and non-Native locals gather for a community potluck.

This crumble, or fruit crisp, uses both honey and maple syrup to sweeten the tart berries and their crunchy cornmeal topping.

SERVES 4 TO 6

Cornmeal Topping
- 1 cup yellow cornmeal
- ½ cup (1 stick) unsalted butter, melted
- ½ cup honey
- ¼ cup maple syrup

Fruit Mixture
- 4 cups fresh or frozen cranberries
- ½ cup honey
- ½ cup maple syrup
- 1 cup sugar

Preheat the oven to 350°F. Butter an 8-inch square baking dish.

For the topping: Put the cornmeal in a medium bowl. Stir in the butter, honey, and maple syrup to make a stiff dough. Set aside.

For the fruit mixture: In a medium saucepan, combine the cranberries, honey, maple syrup, and sugar. Bring to a simmer over medium heat and cook until the berries have started to pop, about 10 minutes. Pour into the prepared dish and drop the dough by tablespoonfuls onto the hot fruit. Bake for 20 to 25 minutes, or until the topping is golden brown.

Remove from the oven and let cool for about 10 minutes. Serve warm.

BREAD PUDDING
WITH CANDIED WALNUTS AND RAISINS

Nuts were a valuable food for Native people throughout many parts of North America: they were ground into butter, dried and ground into flour for breads and cereals, and pounded into a thickening meal for breads and soups. Native cooks may even, as in this recipe, have roasted walnuts with a maple sugar coating to "candy" them.

SERVES 6 TO 8

Candied Walnuts
    ½ cup walnuts
    1 tablespoon water
    3 tablespoons sugar

Bread Pudding
    1 cup heavy cream
    ½ cup apple juice or cider
    ½ cup sugar
    ¼ cup unsalted butter, melted
    3 large eggs
    1 teaspoon ground cinnamon
    ½ teaspoon ground nutmeg
    1 teaspoon vanilla extract
    1 loaf stale country bread or baguette,
        cut into 1-inch cubes (about 6 cups)
    ½ cup raisins

Preheat the oven to 350°F. Butter an 8-inch square baking dish.

For the candied walnuts: Put the nuts in a medium bowl and sprinkle with the water. Toss to coat. Sprinkle with the sugar and toss again. Spread on a rimmed baking sheet and bake for 8 to 10 minutes, or until lightly browned. Remove from the oven and let cool for about 10 minutes; transfer to a bowl.

For the bread pudding: In a large bowl, combine the cream, apple juice or cider, sugar, butter, eggs, spices, and vanilla. Add the bread cubes and stir. Add the candied walnuts and raisins; stir to mix. Pour the mixture into the prepared pan and let stand for about 10 minutes for the bread to absorb the liquid. Bake for 20 to 25 minutes, or until lightly browned and firm to the touch. Remove from the oven and let cool for about 10 minutes. Cut into slices or wedges and serve warm.

MAPLE POPCORN BALLS

Popcorn, one of the oldest species of corn in the world, was so familiar to the Moche people on the northern coast of Peru by about AD 500 that they had devised special pottery containers for popping it over the fire. By the 1500s, an Aztec ceremony to honor the spirit that protected fishermen included scattering pieces of fluffy popped corn at the base of his statue. And legend has it that Chief Massasoit's brother brought to the 1621 Pilgrim Thanksgiving feast a deerskin bag of parched corn, or popcorn. Long before molasses-coated Cracker Jack was invented in Chicago in the 1890s, maple syrup and popcorn had been a familiar combination to Native people in northeastern North America.

MAKES 8 POPCORN BALLS

2 tablespoons canola oil
¼ cup popcorn kernels
1½ cups maple syrup
3 tablespoons unsalted butter

In a large saucepan, heat the oil over medium-high heat until it shimmers. Add the popcorn, cover, and shake the pan back and forth over the burner until all the popcorn has popped. Pour the popcorn into a large bowl and set aside.

In a small saucepan, heat the maple syrup over medium heat until a candy thermometer registers 290°F. Carefully remove from the heat and stir in the butter until it melts. Let cool slightly. Pour over the popcorn and mix with oiled hands. Form the mixture into 8 3-inch balls. As you make them, transfer each to a baking sheet lined with parchment paper to cool. Store in an airtight container for up to 2 days.

Corn and Chocolate Tamales

Corn and Chocolate Tamales

MAKES 10 TAMALES

12 dried corn husks
2 cups masa harina
4 cups milk
1 cup sugar
½ cup chocolate syrup
12 ounces bittersweet chocolate, broken into 1½-inch pieces
½ cup (1 stick) cold unsalted butter, cut into pieces
¼ cup thawed frozen *choclo desgranado* (*see Ingredients and Sources, page 171*) or ½ cup fresh or thawed frozen corn kernels (about 1 ear if fresh)

Soak the corn husks in hot water for 30 minutes. Drain and pat dry. Tear two of the husks into 10 lengthwise strips.

In a large pot, combine the masa harina, milk, sugar, and chocolate syrup. Stir to blend. Bring to a boil over medium-high heat. Reduce the heat to a simmer and cook for 5 to 8 minutes, stirring constantly. Remove from the heat and stir in 1 cup of the chocolate chunks and the butter until melted and smooth. Stir in the *choclo* or corn kernels. Let cool completely.

Lay a corn husk on a work surface and place about ⅓ cup of the masa mixture in the center. Spread the mixture into a rectangle about 2½ inches wide and 3 inches long, leaving a 1½-inch border on the sides and one end of the husk. Place a few of the remaining chocolate chunks in the center of the masa layer. Fold in the sides of the corn husk and then fold the pointed end of the husk over. Fold over the other end and tie closed crosswise with a corn husk strip. Repeat with the remaining corn husks, masa mixture, and chocolate. Refrigerate for at least 30 minutes, or up to 2 days.

Bring 1 cup of water to a brisk simmer in a 6-quart saucepan or stockpot containing a steamer basket. Place the tamales on end in the steamer basket; cover and cook for 20 to 25 minutes, or until heated through.

Developed by the Maya and their Olmec ancestors in Mesoamerica between about 1000 BC and AD 900, chocolate took many forms. For the aristocracy, Maya and Aztec cooks mixed the bitter cacao powder with water and flavored it with spices. For the less elite, cacao was added to maize porridge along with chile or other flavorings. Chocolate in solid form, however, was carried exclusively by Aztec warriors and long-distance traders as part of their fortifying rations, since their professions were considered crucial to the strength of the state.

These dessert tamales combine the old pairing of corn and chocolate in a new way.

Bannock Bread with Berries

There are almost as many variations of bannock bread as there are Native cooks, but whether made with cornmeal or wheat flour, baked in an oven or fried in a cast-iron pan, the bread is an early European adaptation of tribal corn breads (the word *bannock* is Scottish in origin). This sweet version is baked like a shortcake, then topped with sweetened whipped cream and fresh berries.

Serves 4

1 cup all-purpose flour
¼ cup sugar
1¾ teaspoons baking powder
Pinch of salt
3 tablespoons cold unsalted butter
¼ cup ice water
¼ cup heavy cream
2 cups fresh blackberries
2 cups fresh raspberries

Preheat the oven to 350°F. Butter a baking sheet.

In a medium bowl, combine the flour, 2 tablespoons of the sugar, the baking powder, and salt. Stir with a whisk to blend. Using a pastry cutter, cut in the butter until the mixture resembles coarse meal. Using a fork, stir in the cold water just until the dry ingredients begin to come together.

On a floured board, form the dough into a disk. Wrap in plastic wrap and let rest for 15 to 20 minutes.

Roll the dough out to a thickness of ½ inch. Using a 3-inch biscuit cutter, cut out 4 rounds of dough. Transfer the rounds to the prepared pan and bake for 15 to 20 minutes, or until lightly browned. Remove from the oven. Transfer the rounds to a wire rack and let cool slightly.

Meanwhile, in a deep bowl, beat the heavy cream until soft peaks form. Beat in the remaining 2 tablespoons sugar.

To serve, place one round on each of 4 dessert plates and top each serving with whipped cream and berries.

PUMPKIN COOKIES

Whether roasted in hot embers, boiled for soup, sweetened with maple sugar, or incorporated into breads, the flesh of pumpkin and other squashes has long been fundamental to the cooking of Native peoples.

This recipe uses nutmeg and allspice, which is very similar to the native North American spiceberry, to flavor cookies that are rich with dried currants and pumpkin seeds.

MAKES ABOUT 3 DOZEN COOKIES

1 cup sugar
1 cup (2 sticks) unsalted butter at room temperature
1 cup pumpkin puree
1 large egg
1 teaspoon vanilla extract
2 cups all-purpose flour
1 teaspoon baking soda
½ teaspoon salt
½ teaspoon ground nutmeg
¼ teaspoon ground allspice
1 cup dried currants
½ cup pumpkin seeds

Preheat the oven to 350°F. Butter 2 baking sheets.

In a large bowl, beat the sugar and butter together until light and fluffy, about 5 minutes with a handheld mixer at medium speed. Add the pumpkin, egg, and vanilla, and beat until smooth.

In a large bowl, combine the flour, baking soda, salt, nutmeg, and allspice. Stir with a whisk to blend. Gradually stir the wet ingredients into the dry ingredients until smooth. Stir in the currants and pumpkin seeds.

Drop spoonfuls of the batter ½ inch apart on the prepared pans. Bake for 12 to 15 minutes, or until lightly browned. Remove from the oven and let cool on the baking sheets for 5 minutes. Transfer to wire racks to cool completely. Store in an airtight container for up to 5 days.

Drinks

Edward H. Davis (1862–1951). A Mayo mother and boy pose next to large pottery cooking jars, 1924. Sonora State, Mexico. N24767

Irma Rodriguez Moroco (Quechua, b. 1969) and Exaltacion Mamani Amaro (Quechua, b. 1962). Painted pottery qero, 2005. Raqchi, Peru. 21 x 16.4 cm. 26/5293

Sugarcane and Mint Agua Fresca

Known as *aguas frescas* in Mexico and *jugos* throughout much of South America, cold drinks made from water, sugar, and crushed fruit or fruit juice are an integral part of daily life throughout the Western Hemisphere's tropical regions.

This Caribbean version is sweetened with simple syrup and flavored with fresh mint; sugarcane sticks are used as stirrers.

SERVES 6 TO 8

1 cup simple syrup (*page 167*), or to taste
1 cup packed fresh mint leaves
8 cups water
2 pieces sugarcane (*see Ingredients and Sources, page 171*),
    cut into 6 or 8 sticks

In a pitcher, combine the syrup, mint, and water. Stir to dissolve the syrup. Pour into tall glasses over ice and add 1 stick of sugarcane to each glass.

Ella Irving (Oglala Lakota, 1906–1999). Glazed and painted pottery coffee set, 1956–1958. Pine Ridge Reservation, South Dakota. 26/5556

CRANBERRY SPRITZER

Most Native peoples used wild plants and berries to flavor their drinking water. Many of these plants, including cranberries, were tart or bitter, but the bitterness was seen as beneficial, a tonic for the system.

In this recipe, syrup made from cane sugar replaces the maple syrup that Northeast Native cooks might have used to offset the cranberries' natural tartness.

SERVES 4

> 1 cup unsweetened cranberry juice
> ½ cup fresh orange juice
> ½ cup (or to taste) simple syrup (*page 167*)
> 2 cups sparkling water

In a large pitcher, combine the cranberry and orange juices. Stir in the simple syrup until dissolved. Just before serving, stir in the sparkling water.

Serve over ice in tall glasses.

Hibiscus Agua Fresca

Hibiscus Agua Fresca

Infusions of bright red dried hibiscus flowers (also known as *jamaica*) are also the basis for one of the most popular of the cooling *aguas frescas* sold in Mexican cafes and street stands. In the town of Santa María Huatulco in Oaxaca, everyone participates in harvesting the *jamaica* bushes each year, drying the flowers on roofs and patios.

High in vitamin C and vibrant with color, this makes a refreshing summer drink.

Serves 6

> 6 cups water
> 1 cup dried hibiscus flowers (*see Ingredients and Sources, page 171*)
> ¾ cup simple syrup (*page 167*), or to taste

In a medium saucepan, combine the water and hibiscus. Bring to a boil over high heat, then reduce the heat to a simmer and cook for 3 to 5 minutes. Remove from the heat and let cool. Refrigerate until chilled, at least 1 hour, and strain.

Pour the mixture into a pitcher and stir in the syrup until dissolved. Pour into tall glasses over ice and serve.

QUINOA AGUA FRESCA

The people of pre-Contact Mesoamerica and South America depended on a great many grain- and fruit-based drinks and gruels that satisfied both thirst and hunger. In South America, *chicha*, a fermented maize drink that is one of the Americas' earliest alcoholic beverages, is still the most popular of these. In the Andes, where corn cannot grow at the highest altitudes, quinoa is the basis not only of *chicha* but also of many other hot and cold drinks. Incorporating European citrus fruits into an ancient Native recipe, this nonalcoholic version is a true product of a cultural encounter that continues to influence cuisines worldwide.

Three Mesoamerican and South American painted pottery drinking vessels. Clockwise from upper right: Probably Guanacaste-Nicoya jar with rattle legs in the form of a puma, AD 1200–1400. Costa Rica. 26 x 22 x 35.5 cm. 19/4896; probably Moche stirrup-spout vessel depicting a jaguar with its front paws resting on a human figure, 200 BC– AD 100. Peru. 16 x 9 x 19 cm. 5/1888; probably Tiwanaku qero in the form of a puma, AD 600–900. Bolivia. 15 x 22 cm. 20/6314

SERVES 6

½ cup yellow quinoa, rinsed
   (*see Ingredients and Sources, page 171*)
1½ cups water
2 tablespoons sugar, plus ½ cup
1 teaspoon vanilla extract
2 cups fresh orange juice
1 cup fresh lime juice
½ cup fresh lemon juice

In a medium saucepan, combine the quinoa, water, and the 2 tablespoons sugar. Bring to a boil, reduce the heat to a simmer, cover, and cook for 15 minutes, or until the quinoa is translucent and tender. Remove from the heat and let cool for 30 minutes.

In a blender, puree the quinoa mixture in batches. Pour into a large bowl. Stir in the orange, lime, and lemon juices. Stir in the ½ cup sugar until dissolved. Refrigerate until chilled, at least 1 hour.

Serve over ice in tall glasses.

Basic Recipes and Techniques

COURT BOUILLON

MAKES 8 CUPS

8 cups water
1 small carrot, sliced
1 small yellow onion, sliced
1 stalk celery, sliced
1 lemon, halved
½ cup dry white wine
1 fresh thyme sprig
3 peppercorns
1 bay leaf

In a large stockpot, combine all the ingredients. Bring to a boil and cook for 5 minutes. Remove from the heat and strain. Store in the refrigerator for up to 3 days, or freeze for up to 3 months.

Alanson B. Skinner (1886–1925)/Julian A. Dimock (1873–1945). A Seminole woman cooks inside a chickee while another woman, a girl, and a toddler look on, 1910. Big Cypress Swamp, Florida. L00332

VEGETABLE STOCK

MAKES 8 CUPS

2 yellow onions, chopped
3 carrots, peeled and chopped
4 stalks celery, chopped
2 leeks (white part only), rinsed and chopped
4 to 5 ounces button mushrooms, halved
2 portobello mushrooms, quartered
1 teaspoon black peppercorns
4 bay leaves
¼ cup chopped garlic (8 to 10 cloves)
9 cups water

In a stockpot, combine all the ingredients and bring to a boil. Reduce the heat to a simmer and cook for 30 to 40 minutes, or until flavorful and reduced to about 8 cups. Remove from the heat and strain, discarding the vegetables and herbs. Let cool, then cover and refrigerate for up to 3 days, or freeze for up to 3 months.

BLACK BEANS

MAKES 8 CUPS

> 2 cups dried black beans, rinsed
>   and picked over
> ½ onion, quartered
> 1 carrot, peeled, halved, and split horizontally
> 2 stalks celery, cut into 2-inch pieces
> 1 bay leaf

Soak the beans overnight in a large saucepan of water to cover by 2 inches. Drain and add fresh water to cover by 2 inches. Add the remaining ingredients. Bring to a boil, reduce the heat to a simmer, and cook, uncovered, until tender, about 1½ hours. Remove from the heat. Discard the bay leaf and vegetables.

CRANBERRY BEANS

Cranberry beans are also known as Roman or borlotti beans. Although similar to pinto beans, cranberry beans are smaller and firmer, and they tend to keep their shape better in salads.

MAKES 8 CUPS

> 2 cups dried cranberry beans, rinsed and
>   picked over
> 1 yellow onion, chopped
> 1 carrot, peeled and cut into 1-inch slices
> 1 bay leaf

In a large saucepan, soak the beans overnight in water to cover by 2 inches. Drain and add water to cover by 2 inches. Add the onion, carrot, and bay leaf. Bring to a boil over high heat, reduce the heat to a simmer, and cook, uncovered, until tender, about 1½ hours. Remove the bay leaf.

PINTO BEANS

The British and French word *haricot* derives from the Aztec name (*ayecotl*) for the scarlet runner bean, but it now refers to many more bean varieties. Most of the beans that are available in North America and Europe today are the descendants of one species (*Phaseolus vulgaris*) that was first cultivated in Mesoamerica more than 5,000 years ago.

MAKES 4 CUPS

> 1 cup dried pinto beans, rinsed
> and picked over
> ½ yellow onion, diced
> 1 small carrot, peeled and cut into fourths
> 1 bay leaf
> Salt and freshly ground pepper to taste

In a large saucepan, soak the beans overnight in water to cover by 2 inches. Drain and add water to cover by 2 inches. Add the remaining ingredients. Bring to a boil over high heat, reduce the heat to low, and cook, uncovered, until the beans are tender, about 1½ hours. Remove the bay leaf and carrot. Season with salt and pepper.

TOASTING NUTS AND SEEDS

Preheat the oven to 350°F. Spread the nuts or seeds on a rimmed baking sheet and toast until lightly browned and fragrant, about 8 minutes. Pour into a bowl and let cool.

For hazelnuts: After toasting, pour the nuts onto a dish towel, fold the towel closed, and rub to remove the hazelnut skins.

ROASTING CHILES AND PEPPERS

Preheat broiler. Place chiles or peppers on a broiler pan and broil as close to the heating element as possible, turning with tongs to blacken them on all sides. Transfer to a bowl, cover with plastic wrap, and let cool to the touch, about 10 minutes. Peel or rub off the skin. Seed and core the chiles, then cut them as described in the main recipe.

SIMPLE SYRUP

In a large saucepan, combine 1 cup sugar and 1 cup water. Bring to a boil over high heat, stirring until the sugar dissolves. Reduce the heat to a simmer and cook for 1 minute. Remove from the heat and let cool. Cover and store in the refrigerator indefinitely. Makes about 1⅓ cups.

ACKNOWLEDGMENTS

Like running the Mitsitam Cafe, compiling this cookbook was a collaborative process. I would first and foremost like to thank the staff at Restaurant Associates, who have helped keep the cafe working smoothly 364 days a year for the past six years, especially chefs Bruce Barnes and Nathaniel Auchter, regional director George Conomos, and cafe director Jaimmey Holmes.

Many thanks, too, to restaurant consultants Fernando and Marlene Divina, who conceptualized and planned the cafe, and to Duane Blue Spruce (Laguna/Ohkay Owingeh), formerly the museum's architectural liaison, who played a key role in its construction.

I am grateful to Kevin Gover (Pawnee), the director of the National Museum of the American Indian, and Tim Johnson (Mohawk), the associate director for museum programs, for their unwavering and essential support for this book as it evolved.

A big thanks to the museum's Publications Office, including publications manager Tanya Thrasher (Cherokee Nation of Oklahoma), managing editor Ann Kawasaki, and Sally Barrows, the book's project editor, who researched the recipe notes and put all the pieces together. Special thanks to Nicolasa I. Sandoval (Chumash) for her warm and thoughtful introduction.

Women cooking salmon near Annie Garrison's home on the Muckleshoot Reservation, Auburn, Washington, ca. 1950. Courtesy of the Seattle Post-Intelligencer Collection, Museum of History and Industry, Seattle, and the Muckleshoot Indian Tribe. All rights reserved. Left to right: Alice Williams, Annie Garrison, Nevah Jackson Moses, Genevieve Siddle John, Elivna (Bena) Williams, Laura Siddle Courville, and Irene Siddle.

In adapting the cafe's recipes for home cooks, I received invaluable help from editor Carolyn Miller and a team of sixty museum staff people who volunteered to test the recipes in their home kitchens. Their enthusiasm and thoughtful evaluations contributed greatly to the final text.

For the book's terrific food photographs, I am grateful for the teamwork, attention to detail, and unfailing good humor of photographer Renée Comet, stylist Lisa Cherkasky, and assistants Audrey Weppler, Mara Block, and Katie Norwood. Thanks, too, to Olivia Cadaval, Shirley Cherkasky, Mara Cherkasky, Claire Cherkasky, José Montaño (Aymara), Ben Norman (Pamunkey), and the Sur la Table store for their help in supplying table- and dishware.

I would also like to acknowledge the tireless work of Cindy Frankenburg, Ernest Amoroso, Katherine Fogden (Mohawk), Walter Larrimore, and Roger A. Whiteside of NMAI's Photo Services Department. Extra thanks to Lou Stancari of NMAI's Photo Archives Department and Alyssa Reiner at the Smithsonian's Office of Contracting.

In addition, a big thanks to Derek Lawrence, Katie Wensuc, Katie O'Neill, and Faith Marcovecchio at Fulcrum Publishing and Margaret McCullough of Corvus Design Studio for creating a beautiful book and publishing it with savvy and attention to detail.

Lastly, I thank the cafe's customers, whose willingness to explore the Americas' indigenous foods and requests for recipes directly inspired me to write this book.

—RICHARD HETZLER

INGREDIENTS AND SOURCES

This list describes some of the recipe ingredients with which you may be unfamiliar or that you may have trouble finding at your local supermarket. Most of the ingredients in this section are available at specialty markets and some are available online. For a list of websites from which some of these foods may be ordered, see Online Suppliers, page 174.

Ají amarillo: *Ají* is the term for "chile" in the Quechua language and refers to at least 24 different varieties. Most commonly used in Peru is the medium-hot yellow ají amarillo. It is available in powder or paste form at some Latino markets.

Ají limo: A dried red or yellow Peruvian chile. Available in powder form in small packages at some Latino markets. Cayenne pepper may be substituted.

Ají panco: This large red chile is one of the most popularly used in Peru. Available in both paste and powder form in Latino markets.

Anaheim chile: This long chile may be either green or red, fresh or dried. The red Anaheim is also known as *chile colorado.*

Ancho chile: The poblano chile, when allowed to ripen to red and then dried, becomes the ancho chile. Dark red and triangle-shaped, it is the most popular chile in Mexico. Look for it in Latino markets.

Arepa flour: A precooked "instant" corn flour for making arepas, found in Latino markets. Yellow arepa flour has more flavor than white.

Banana leaves: The large green leaves of the banana tree are widely used throughout the tropics as a wrap for foods to be grilled or roasted. Available in Latino and Asian markets.

Black mustard seeds: Popular in East Indian cuisine, these are more pungent than yellow mustard seeds. Available in natural foods stores and Indian markets.

Blue cornmeal: A dark blue-gray cornmeal made from the blue corn popular in the Southwest. Available in natural foods and specialty foods stores as well as Latino markets.

Buffalo (bison) meat: Low in fat and rich in iron, buffalo meat is a flavorful alternative to beef. Order it from your butcher or online. Available in some grocery stores.

Celery root (celeriac): A round, knobby, brown root available in most regions of United States in winter. Celery root must be peeled, but the crisp white interior flesh is good raw, in a variety of salads.

Chayote: Known also as christophine, mirliton, and vegetable pear, the pale green pear-shaped chayote has a mild flavor and smooth flesh. Look for it in Latino markets and specialty produce stores.

Chestnut puree: Canned, unsweetened chestnut puree is available in some specialty markets.

Chipotle chile: The smoked dried jalapeño chile. It is available in its dried form in Latino markets, or canned in adobo sauce (chipotle chiles en adobo) in many supermarkets.

Choclo desgranado: A starchy South American corn with large kernels; it is available frozen in some Latino markets.

Corn husks, dried: Used as a wrapper for tamales, dried corn husks are first soaked to become pliable. Found in Latino markets.

Dandelion greens: Long, serrated green leaves, picked in spring for salads and cooked dishes. Found in farmers' markets and many supermarkets.

Duck breast, smoked: Smoked duck breasts are available in some specialty markets.

Epazote: Also known as Mexican tea and wormseed, this herb has long, serrated leaves and a smell that has been compared to both gasoline and mint. It is available both fresh and dried in many Latino markets, and is traditionally used in bean dishes.

Green papaya: The unripe papaya, with a bright, uniformly green skin, crisp white flesh, and white seeds. It has a fresh, acidic taste and is available in Latino markets.

Guajillo chile: A long, narrow brownish red dried chile popular in Mexico. Found in Latino markets.

Habanero chile: This very hot lantern-shaped chile may be available green, but it is usually sold in its ripe orange state. Found in specialty produce stores and Latino markets.

Hen-of-the-woods (maitake) mushroom: A dark brown-gray mushroom that grows in clusters; it is popular in Japanese cuisine. Available in the fall in some specialty foods stores.

Hibiscus flowers (jamaica), dried: These dark red flowers become a nutritious bright red tea or cold drink when brewed. Available in packets in natural foods stores and Latino markets.

Hominy (pozole): Dried white corn kernels that have been soaked in slaked lime or lye to remove their hulls. Dried or canned hominy is available in Latino markets.

Huckleberry: A wild, dark blue berry that resembles the blueberry but is smaller. Available canned or frozen in specialty foods stores and some supermarkets.

Juniper berries, dried: Pungent blue-black fruits of the juniper tree add a woodsy flavor to foods. Available at natural foods stores and specialty foods markets.

Mango, green: The unripe mango is eaten raw with salt and lime in South America; it may also be pickled or cooked. Found in specialty produce markets and Latino markets.

Masa harina: Flour made from corn kernels cooked in lime water, ground into masa (dough), and dried. Used to make tortillas and tamales as an alternative to fresh masa dough. Available in Latino markets and some supermarkets.

Mustard greens: The leaves of mustard greens may appear crumpled or flat, with edges that can be toothed, scalloped, or frilly. They have a pungent, peppery flavor and are available fresh in gourmet and farmers' markets from December through March. You may also find them in the frozen foods section of some supermarkets.

New Mexico chile: A long, fresh chile, it may be either green or red. Both colors can vary in heat from mild to hot. Found in specialty produce stores and Latino markets.

Pasilla chile: A long, narrow, almost-black dried chile, also called *chile negro*. The name *pasilla* is sometimes mistakenly used for the poblano chile in northern Mexico and California. Available in Latino markets.

Poblano chile: A large, blackish green triangle-shaped fresh chile, the poblano is mildly hot. It is almost always roasted and peeled before being cooked. Mistakenly called the pasilla chile in California and northern Mexico, when ripened and dried the poblano becomes the ancho chile. Available in Latino markets and many supermarkets.

Prickly pear puree: The pureed red fruit of the prickly pear cactus. Available in most Latino markets.

Purple potatoes: With a dark purple-blue skin and flesh, these potatoes are a dramatic and colorful addition to many dishes. Found in specialty foods stores and Latino markets.

Quahog: A large hard-shell clam from the East Coast. Found in many fish markets; other large clams may be substituted.

Quinoa: The seed of an Andean plant, quinoa is higher in protein than any other grain. It is available in white and yellow in natural foods stores, and in red and black in specialty foods markets.

Serrano chile: A green or red fresh chile, the serrano is shorter than the jalapeño but also hotter. Widely available in supermarkets and Latino markets.

Sugarcane: The boiled stalks of the sugarcane plant. Found in specialty foods stores and Latino markets. Peel before eating.

Sunchoke (Jerusalem artichoke): The knobby tuber of a variety of sunflower, its flesh is white and crisp when raw, starchy and tender when cooked. Found in specialty produce stores and many supermarkets.

Tamarind pulp: Made from the fruit of a tree that grows worldwide in tropical climates, tamarind pulp is used in both Latino and South Asian cooking. Jellylike and acidic, it is usually sweetened and/or combined with other ingredients in desserts, drinks, and chutneys. Tamarind pulp is available in most Latino and Asian markets.

Venison: Low in fat and high in flavor, farmed venison is available on order from some butchers. See also Online Suppliers, page 174.

Wakame seaweed: A dried seaweed available in Asian markets.

Wild rice: The seed of a wild grass, wild rice is still harvested in the traditional Native way in the northern Great Lakes area. Available in specialty foods markets.

Yuca: The sweet variety of this starchy root, native to South America, is available year-round in Latino and Asian markets and some supermarkets.

Zucchini blossoms: Organic zucchini blossoms are available at some specialty foods markets and some farmers' markets in late spring and throughout the summer.

ONLINE SUPPLIERS

This is an incomplete list of websites from which some of the less easily found ingredients in this book may be ordered. As a guideline, we have listed some of the specific foods that may be available from each company.

www.americanspice.com
Black mustard seeds

www.cookingpost.com
Blue cornmeal

www.dartagnan.com
Venison, smoked duck breast, buffalo (bison)

www.ecuadorianfooddelivery.com
Fresh and frozen yuca root

www.fossilfarms.com
Venison, buffalo (bison)

www.gourmetsleuth.com
Banana leaves, tamarind pulp, dried hibiscus flowers, dried chiles, unsweetened chestnut puree

www.kalustyans.com
Ají amarillo chiles, wakame seaweed, quinoa (white, yellow, red, and black)

www.marxfoods.com
Dried ají limo chiles, hen-of-the-woods (maitake) mushrooms

www.nativeharvest.com/catalog
Native-harvested wild rice

www.nwwildfoods.com
Frozen and canned huckleberries

www.penzeys.com
Dried juniper berries, dried epazote

www.perfectpuree.com
Prickly pear puree

Selected Bibliography

Coe, Sophie D. *America's First Cuisines*. Austin: University of Texas Press, 1994.

Coe, Sophie D., and Michael D. Coe. *The True History of Chocolate*. New York: Thames & Hudson, 2000.

Connell, K. H. "The History of the Potato." *Economic History Review*, New Series, 3, no. 3 (1951): 388–395.

Cox, Beverly, and Martin Jacobs. *Spirit of the Harvest: North American Indian Cooking*. New York: Stewart, Tabori & Chang, 1991.

———. *Spirit of the Earth: Native Cooking from Latin America*. New York: Stewart, Tabori & Chang, 2001.

———. *Body, Mind, and Spirit: Native Cooking of the Americas*. Phoenix: *Native Peoples* magazine, 2004.

Davidson, Alan, ed. *The Oxford Companion to Food*. Oxford: Oxford Univ. Press, 1999.

Densmore, Frances. *How Indians Use Wild Plants for Food, Medicine, and Crafts*. New York: Dover Publications, 1974.

Divina, Fernando, and Marlene Divina. *Foods of the Americas: Native Recipes and Traditions*. Washington, D.C., and Berkeley: National Museum of the American Indian and Ten Speed Press, 2004.

Frank, Lois Ellen. *Foods of the Southwest Indian Nations*. Berkeley: Ten Speed Press, 2002.

Fussell, Betty. *The Story of Corn: The Myths and History, the Culture and Agriculture, the Art and Science of America's Quintessential Crop*. New York: Knopf, 1992.

Hesse, Zora. *Southwestern Indian Recipe Book: Apache, Pima, Papago, Pueblo, and Navajo*. Palmer Lake, CO: Filter Press, 1998.

Johnson, Sylvia A. *Tomatoes, Potatoes, Corn, and Beans: How the Foods of the Americas Changed Eating around the World*. New York: Atheneum Books for Young Readers, 1997.

Kavasch, E. Barrie. *Native Harvests: American Indian Wild Foods and Recipes*. 1979. Revised and expanded second edition (1998) reprinted with a new preface and additional illustrations. Mineola, NY: Dover Publications, 2005.

Kennedy, Diana. *The Art of Mexican Cooking: Traditional Mexican Cooking for Aficionados*. New York: Bantam Books, 1989.

Kijac, Maria Baez. *The South American Table: The Flavor and Soul of Authentic Home Cooking from Patagonia to Rio de Janeiro, with 450 Recipes*. Boston: Harvard Common Press, 2003.

Kimball, Yeffe, and Jean Anderson. *The Art of American Indian Cooking: Over 150 Delicious, Authentic, and Traditional Dishes from Five North American Regions*. Guilford, CT: Lyons Press, 1965.

Luard, Elisabeth. *The Latin American Kitchen*. San Diego: Laurel Glen Publishing, 2002.

Mills, Earl, Sr., and Betty Breen. *Cape Cod Wampanoag Cookbook: Wampanoag Indian Recipes, Images, and Lore.* Santa Fe: Clear Light Publishers, 2001.

National Museum of the American Indian. *Listening to Our Ancestors: The Art of Native Life along the North Pacific Coast.* Washington, D.C.: National Museum of the American Indian and National Geographic, 2005.

National Society for American Indian Elderly. *Wisdom of the Elders: Traditional American Indian Food and Recipes.* Phoenix: National Society for American Indian Elderly, 2006.

Sharpe, J. Ed, and Thomas B. Underwood. *American Indian Cooking and Herb Lore.* Cherokee, NC: Cherokee Publications, 1973.

Snell, Alma Hogan. *A Taste of Heritage: Crow Indian Recipes and Herbal Medicines.* Lincoln: Univ. of Nebraska Press, 2006.

Suttles, Wayne, ed. *Northwest Coast.* Vol. 7, *Handbook of North American Indians,* edited by William C. Sturtevant. Washington, D.C.: Smithsonian Institution, 1990.

Ulmer, Mary, and Samuel E. Beck. *Cherokee Cooklore: Preparing Cherokee Foods.* Cherokee, NC: Museum of the Cherokee Indian, 1951.

Watts, Dolly, and Annie Watts. *Where People Feast: An Indigenous People's Cookbook.* Vancouver, BC: Arsenal Pulp Press, 2007.

Waugh, F. W. *Iroquois Foods and Food Preparation.* Canada Department of Mines, 1916. Reprint, Ohsweken, ON: Iroqrafts Iroquois Reprints, 1991.

Wilson, Gilbert L. *Buffalo Bird Woman's Garden: Agriculture of the Hidatsa Indians.* 1917. Reprint, St. Paul: Minnesota Historical Society Press, 1987.

RECIPES BY NATIVE AMERICAN CULTURE AREA

Great Plains

INDEX

ABOUT THE AUTHOR

© *Smithsonian Institution*

The kitchen of Richard Hetzler's German American childhood home in Baltimore provided his earliest culinary inspiration. After working in restaurant kitchens in high school, Hetzler attended the Baltimore International Culinary College, graduating in 1995. He worked at several fine-dining restaurants in the Washington, D.C., and Baltimore area before joining the food-service firm Restaurant Associates, becoming the executive chef at the Smithsonian National Museum of Natural History. In 2003, he was on the team that researched and developed the groundbreaking concept for the National Museum of the American Indian's Mitsitam Cafe: serving indigenous foods that are the staples of five Native culture areas in North and South America. As the executive chef of the Mitsitam, he has continued to create and refine seasonal menus that showcase the truly native bounty of the Americas.